AF251001

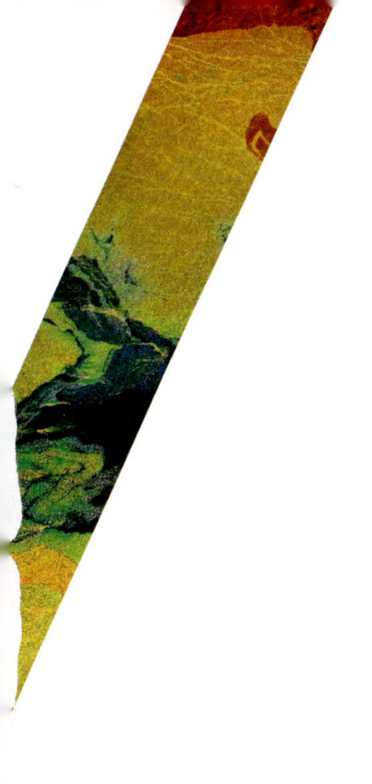

GOWANUS WATERS

STEVEN HIRSCH

INTRODUCTION BY JORDAN G. TEICHER

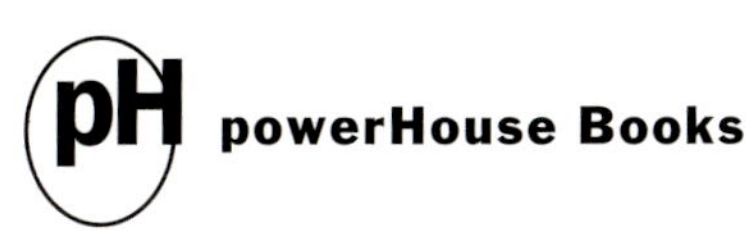

pH powerHouse Books

BROOKLYN, NY

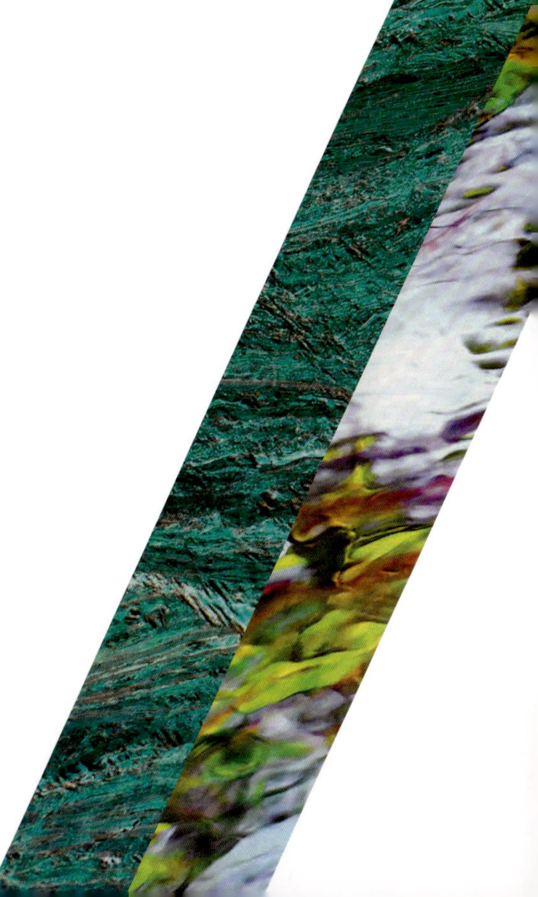

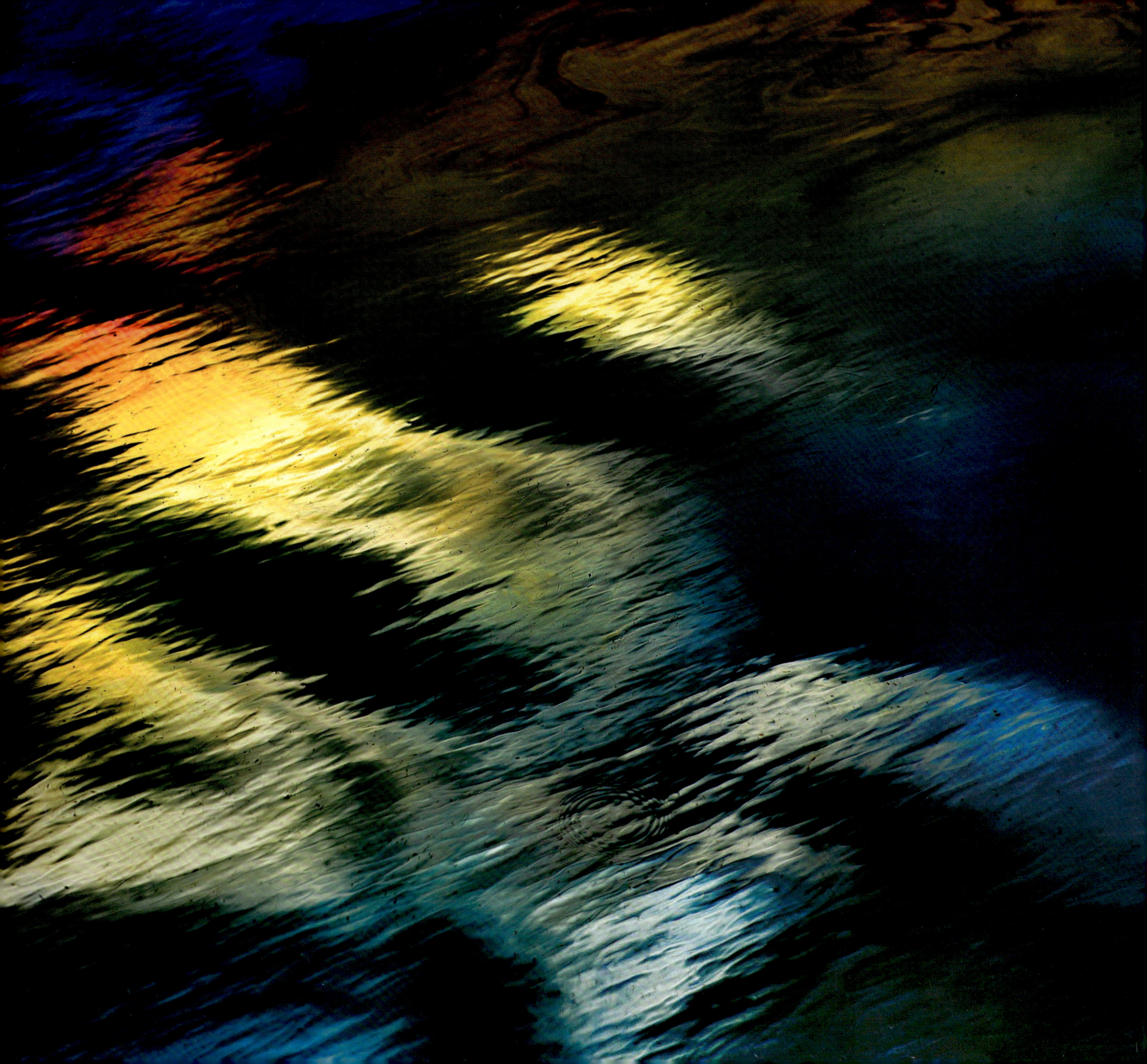

INTRODUCTION

BY JORDAN G. TEICHER

Photography, as a medium, may be intrinsically concerned with time, but abstract photography is something of an anomaly: it is interested in composition rather than record, the essence of something rather than its reality. Steven Hirsch's photographs of the Gowanus Canal, which focus on the ageless qualities of an environmental phenomenon rooted in a specific time and space, fall curiously between these opposing notions.

On certain days at particular points along the 1.8-mile-long waterway that snakes through Brooklyn to the New York Harbor, a combination of ancient industrial pollutants and modern waste gives way to a magnificent rainbow tapestry on the water's surface. This is what Hirsch noticed walking along the canal's banks one day a few years ago and what has intrigued him ever since.

Hirsch's images are as untamed as the canal itself, subject to variations in color, shape, pattern, and texture that reflect the wild waterscape. At their busiest, they are kaleidoscopic images whose elements resemble the spiral arrangements of meteorological events or celestial bodies, and sometimes channel 1960s psychedelic motifs. At their sparest, they look like minimalist exercises in drip painting. The photographs are united in their top-down perspective and close crop; otherwise, one is as different as the next.

Abstract photographers have long turned to nature for raw material. Alfred Stieglitz, for one, photographed clouds in his 1920s series, "Equivalents," as a way to visualize his own interior psychology. But Hirsch's view of the Gowanus promises no such metaphor. If anything, his work has more in common with that of the English botanist Anna Atkins, whose mid-19th-century cyanotypes of algae, which were intended as illustrations for scientific reference, are today appreciated for their abstract, formal elegance.

Hirsch has no documentary or scientific ambitions. Rather, his journey here is exclusively and unapologetically an aesthetic one. Like many abstract photographers, his work depicts an actual, known entity, but it is merely a means to an end — an expression of what Lyle Rexer, in his book, *The Edge of Vision,* identifies as "eternity, atemporality, changelessness beyond change."

In keeping, Hirsch's series is devoid of narrative, and, for the most part, visual context: if he didn't reveal their location, we'd have no way to know the images derived from one of the foulest waterways in the United States. And yet, curiously, while Hirsch's photos may concern what is timeless, his subject is an ephemeral occurrence, a momentary bubbling of oily sludge at the water's surface whose appearance is unpredictable and brief, dependent on specific and relatively rare weather conditions. As a result, to make these photos, Hirsch had to draw on his experience as a New York photojournalist, one whose decades of doggedly photographing the people and streets of the city for tabloid newspapers has made him a skilled hunter of fleeting moments.

On the other hand, no matter how quick he may be, the occurrence Hirsch has photographed is likely endangered. One spring day, we visited the canal and Hirsch saw, for the first time, the water teeming with tiny fish, but caught virtually none of the slime he'd been hoping to discover to make new photographs. Indeed, thanks to its Superfund status, the canal — long referred to by locals as "Lavender Lake" for its distinctive, unnatural hues — is slowly on the mend. Soon enough, Hirsch's polluted palette will be a memory, much like the industrial heyday of the borough's interior.

Talk to Hirsch about the canal and you surely won't hear any of the reverence for nature or concern for the environment that you would from staff at the

Gowanus Canal Conservancy. Hirsch doesn't mourn the canal's changes, but he doesn't advocate for them either. Still, the Gowanus in its current, polluted form is a remnant of a grittier era in New York's history, an attribute Hirsch sees less and less of in this increasingly sanitized city.

Hirsch was born in Williamsburg and now lives in the East Village, and like many who grew up in New York in the last half century, the city he sees today is not like the one in which he was raised. In Hirsch's earlier work – his portraits of defendants at the Manhattan Criminal Court, for instance, or those of Tompkins Square Park's tattooed, vagabond crustpunks – one sees his search for fragments of a city closer to the one he knew, a place more colorful than clean.

Hirsch has found such a symbol, if unwittingly, in the Gowanus. And though the sludge may well dissipate, Hirsch's eye for abstraction will find other treasure troves – he's become fond of dumpsters lately – in parts of New York that would go unnoticed by the rest of us. With any luck, the city will always be dirty somewhere, and always beautiful.

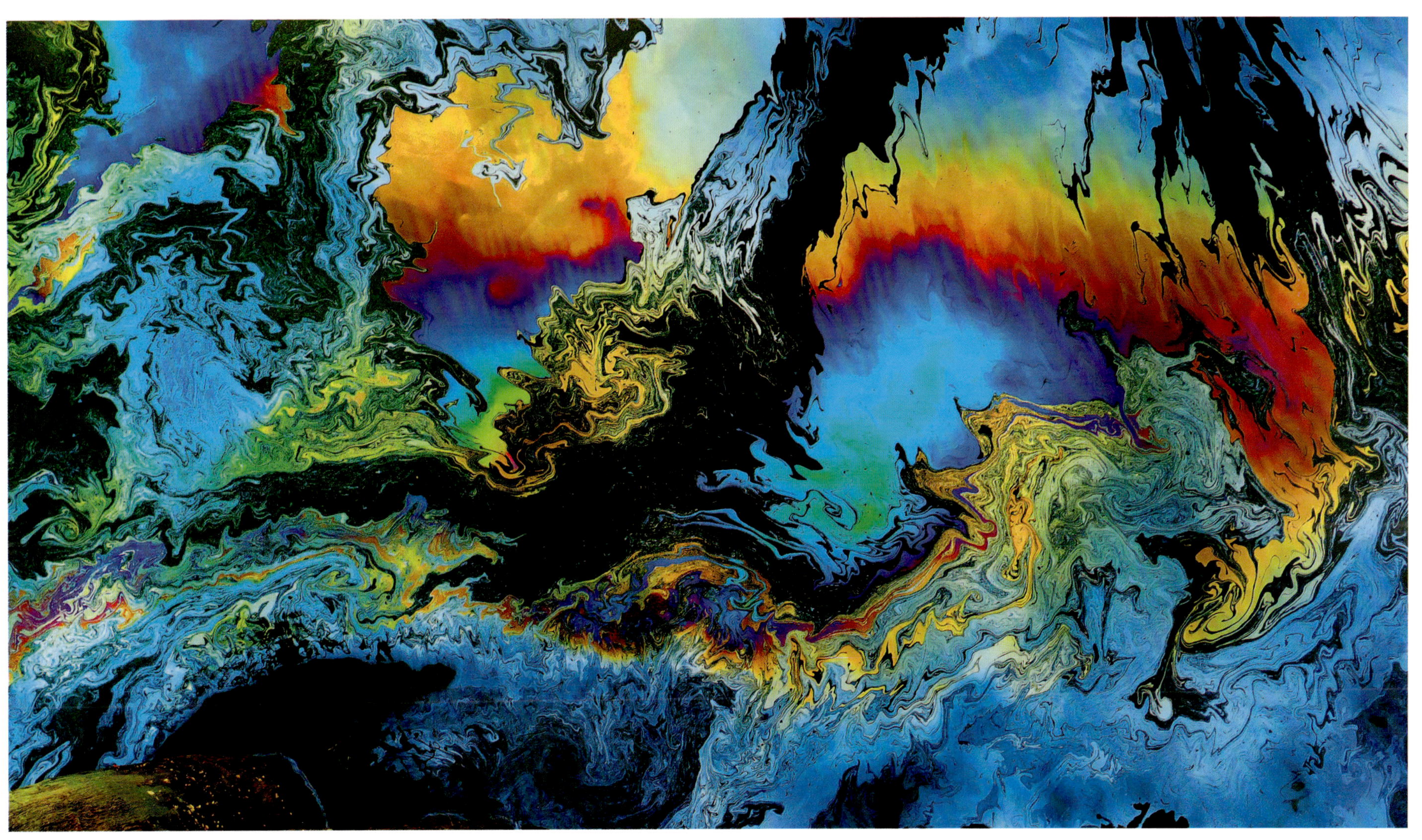

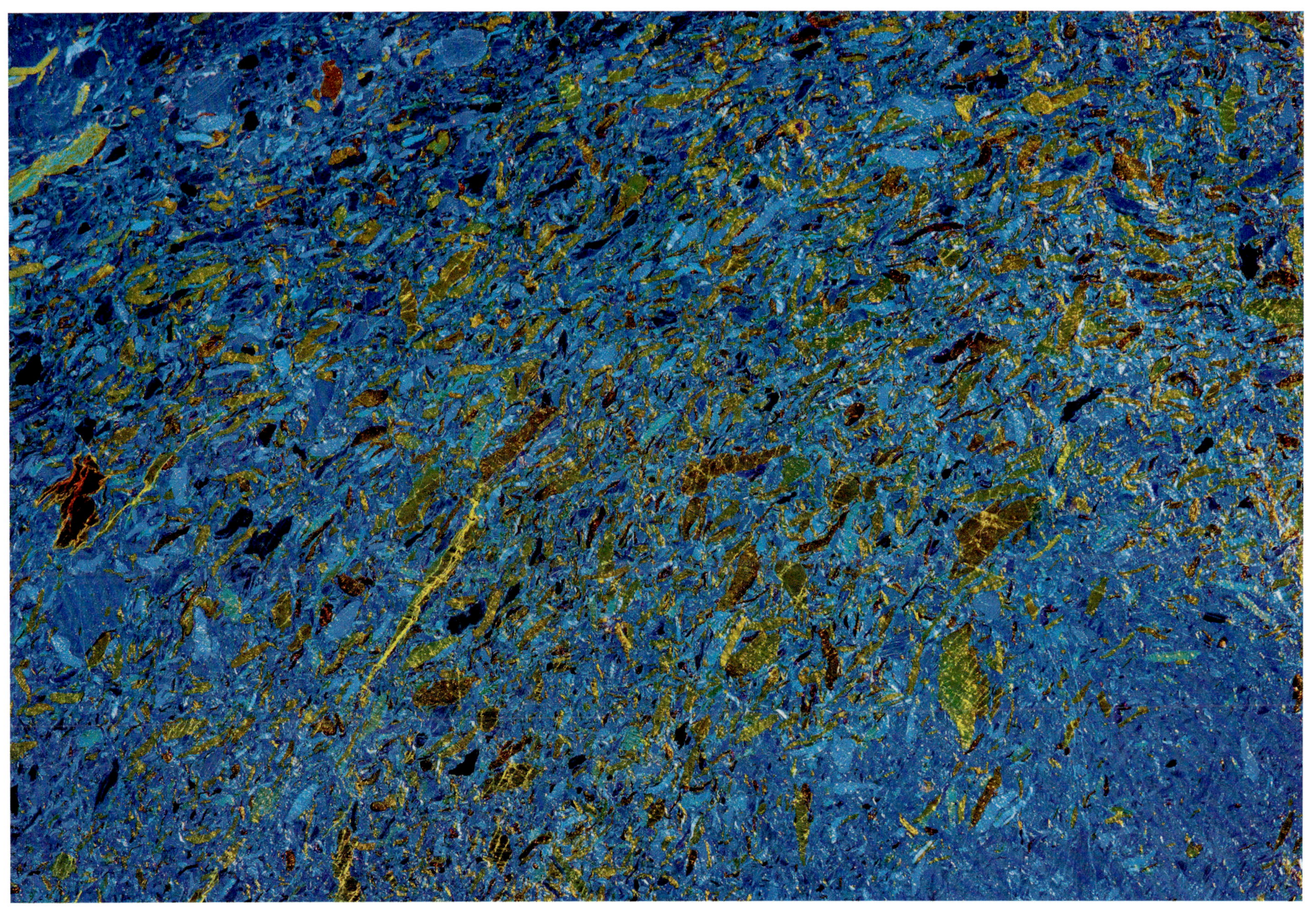

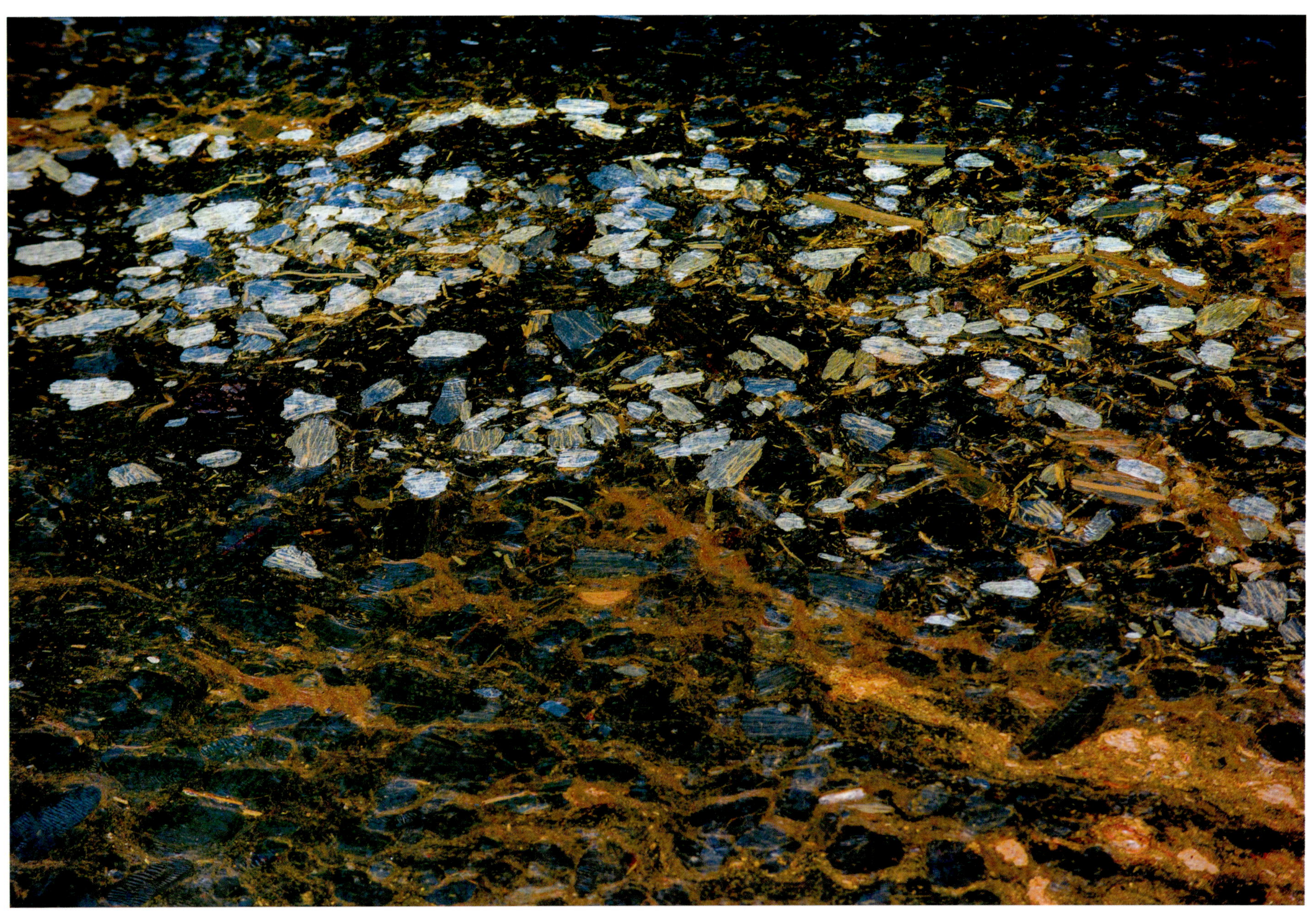

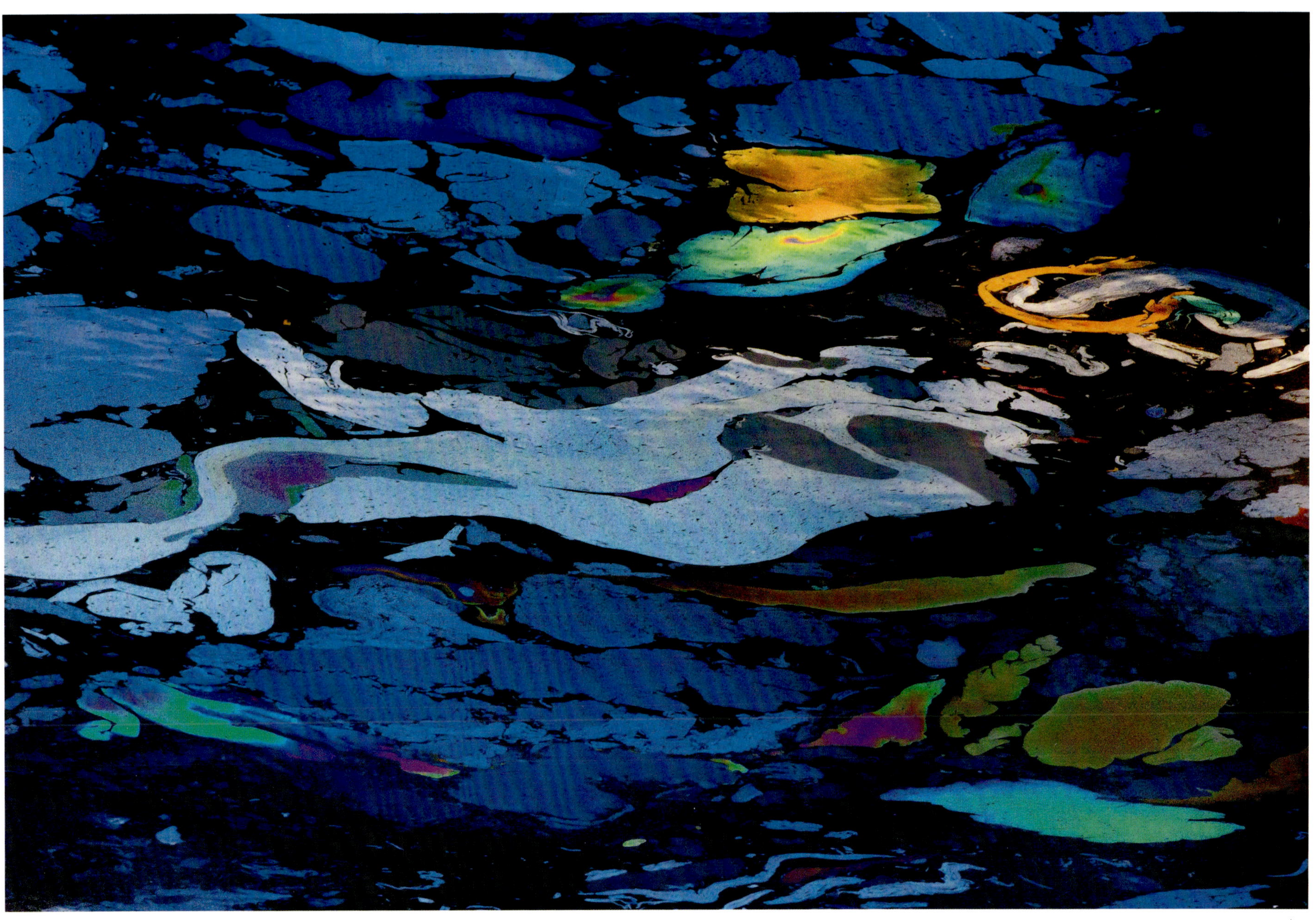

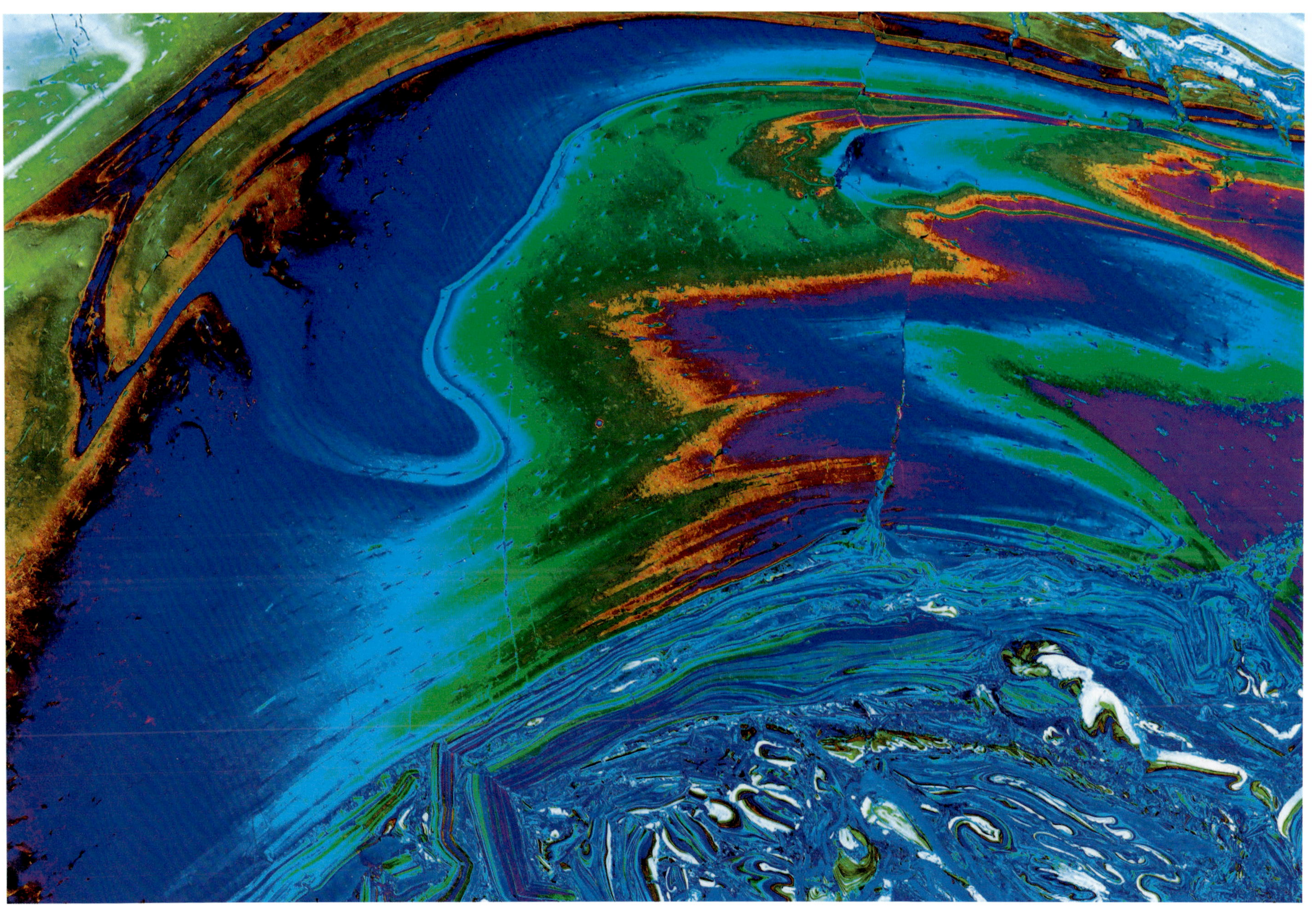

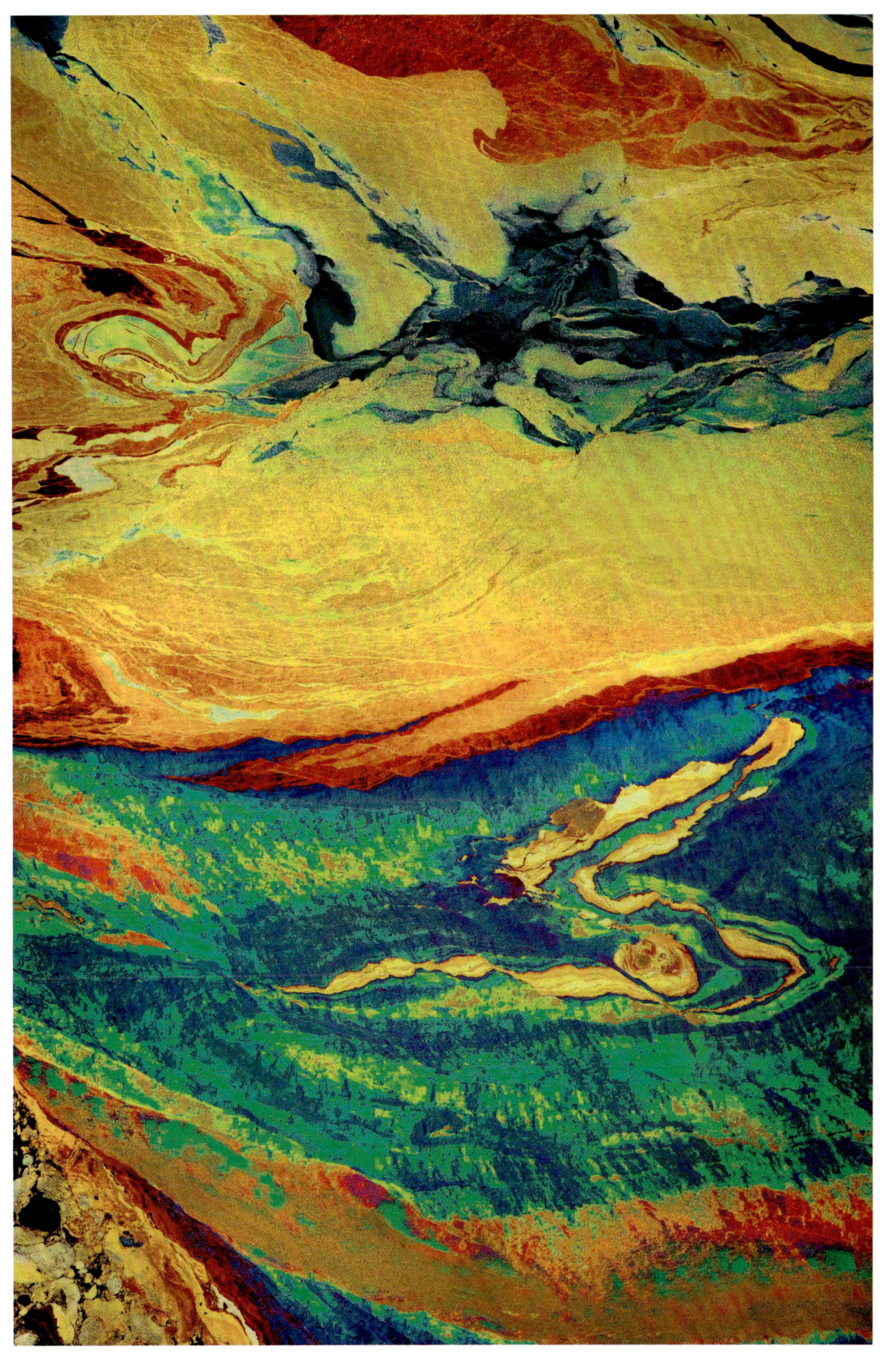

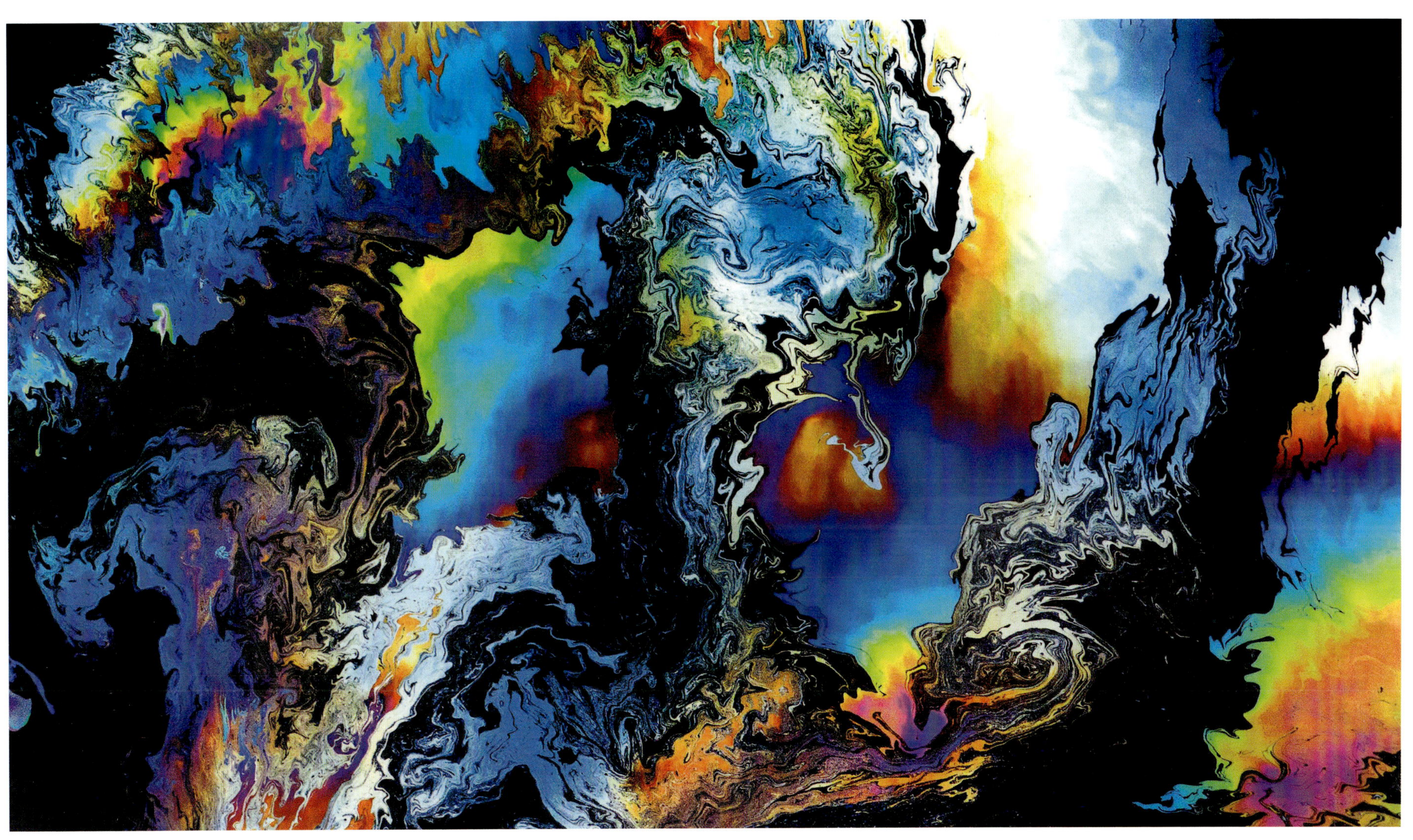

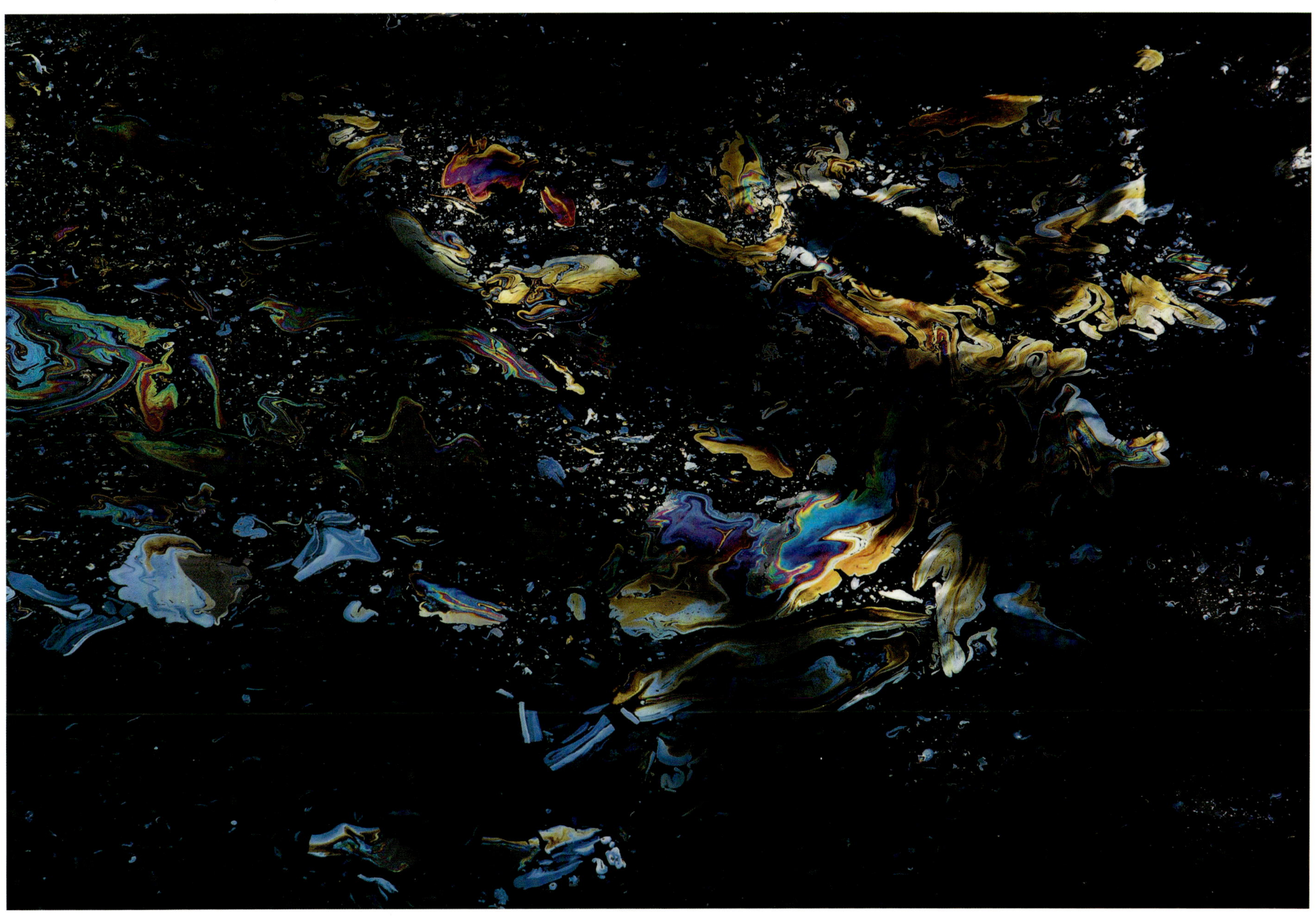

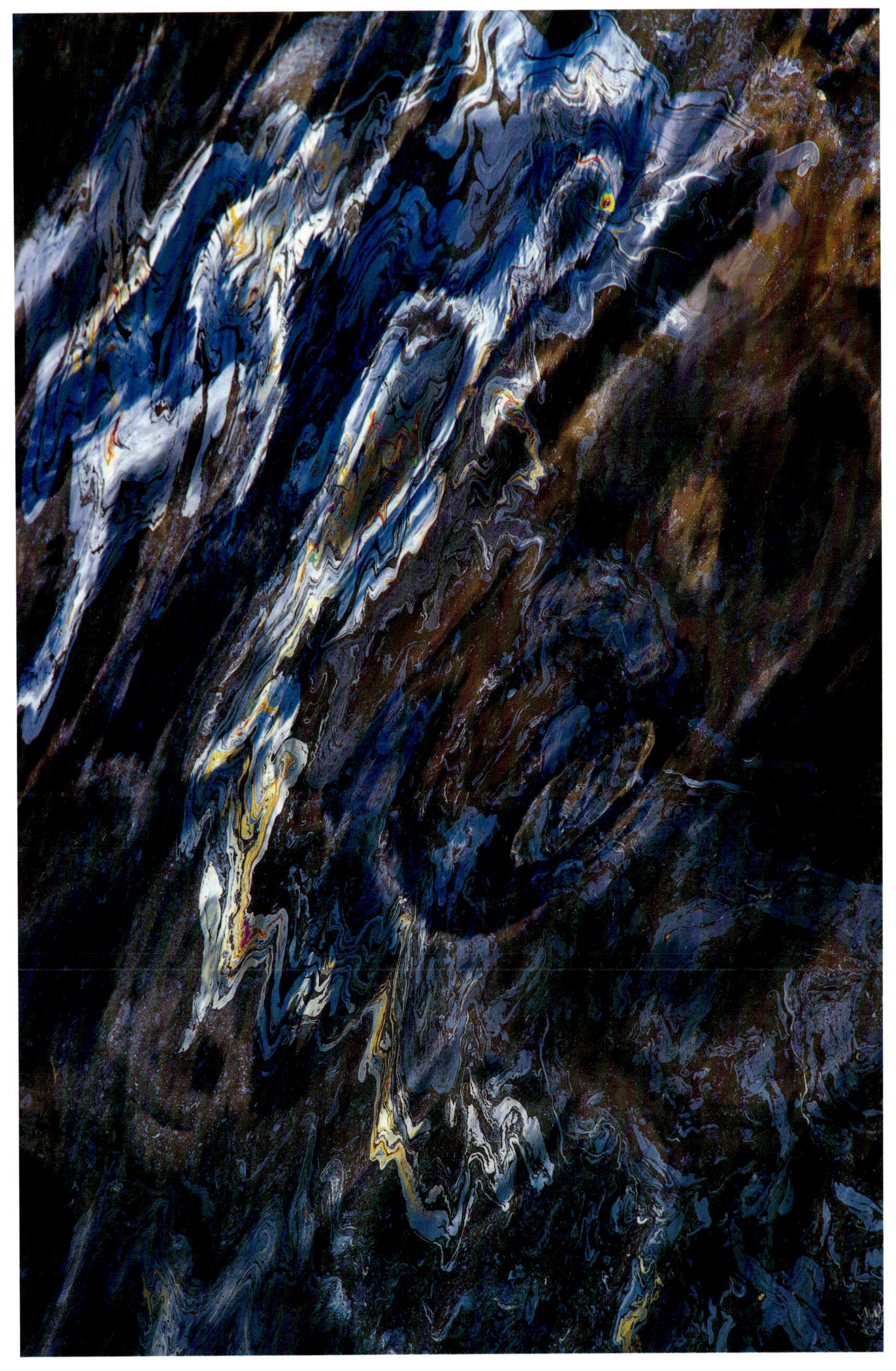

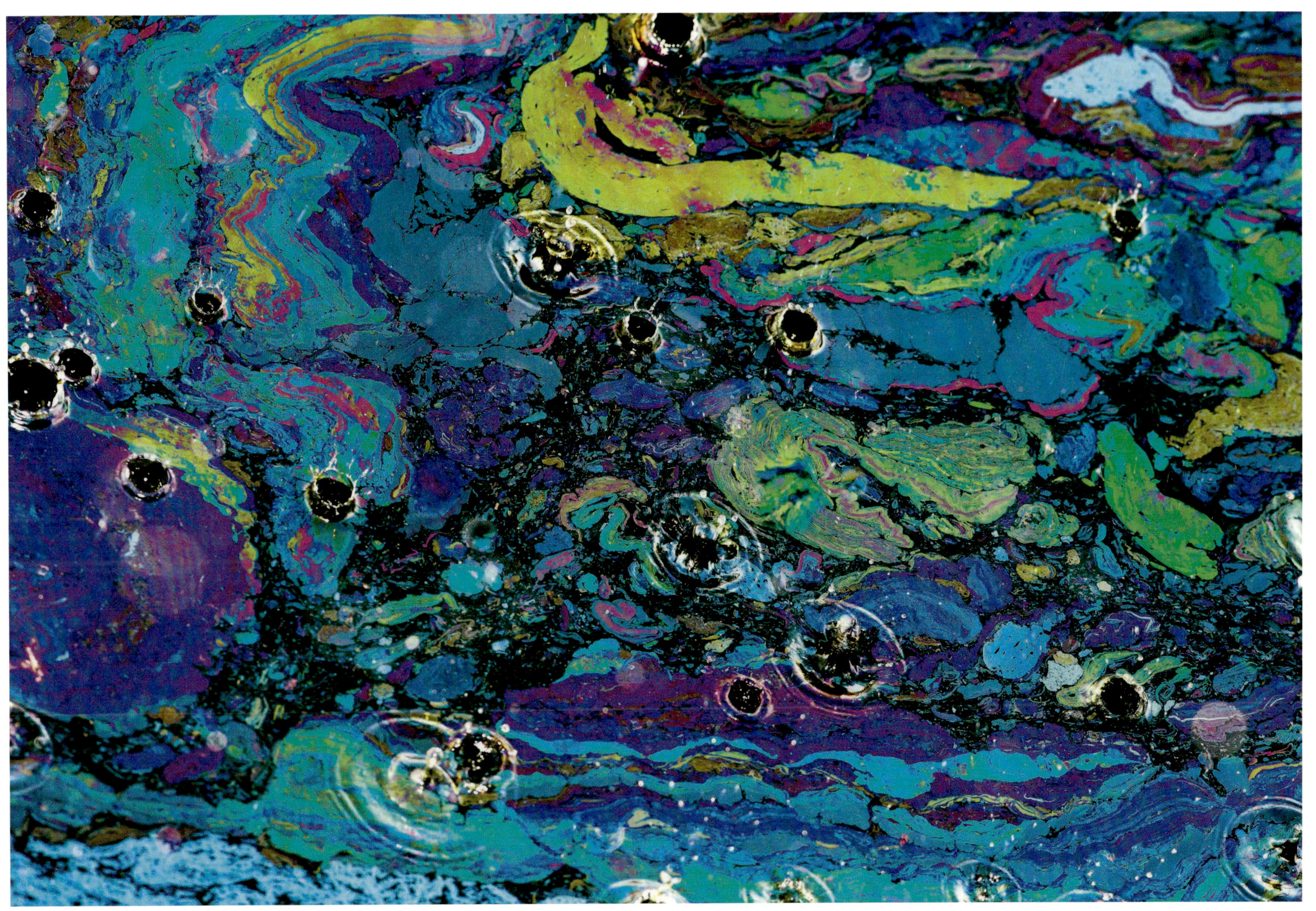

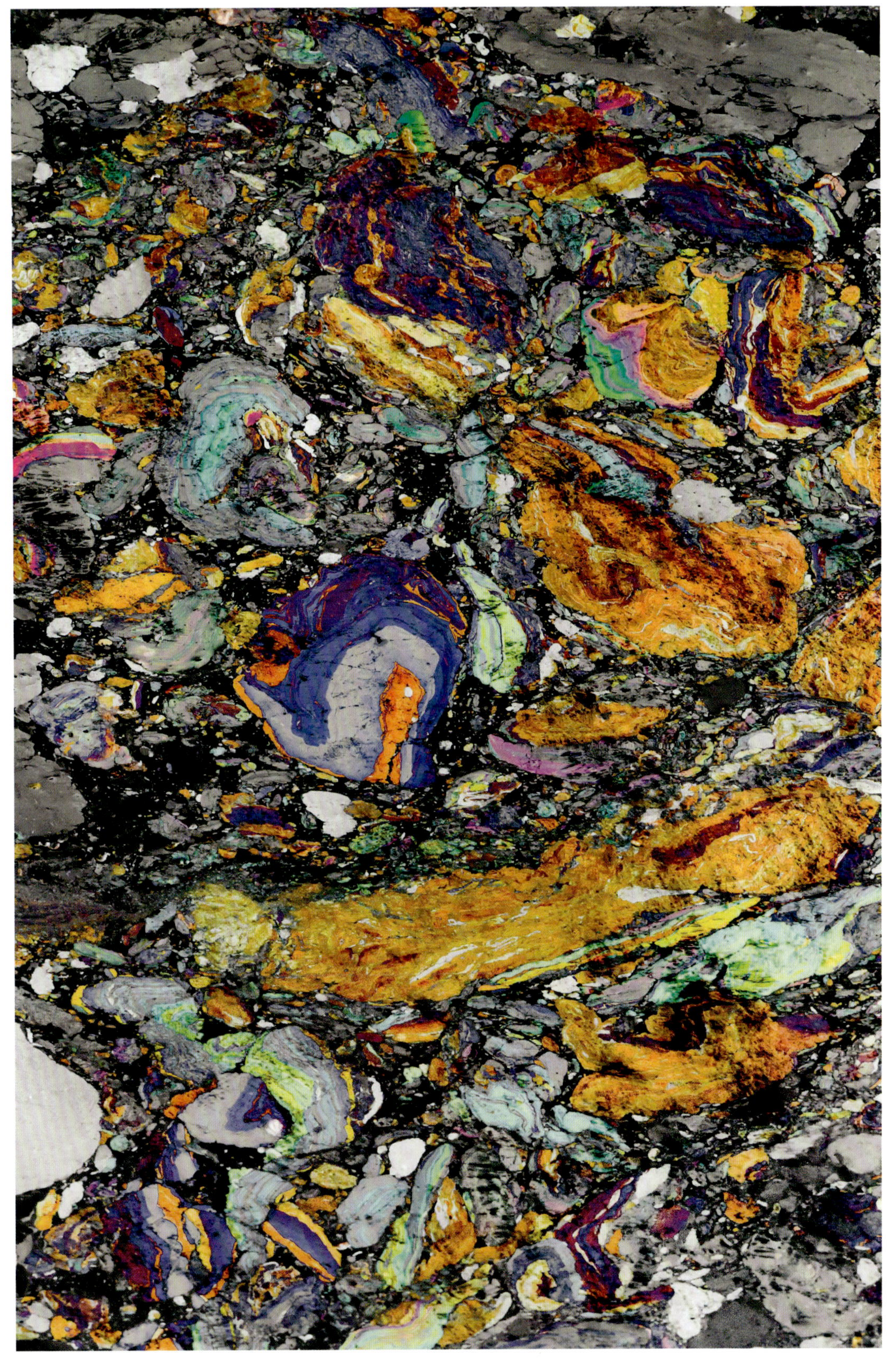

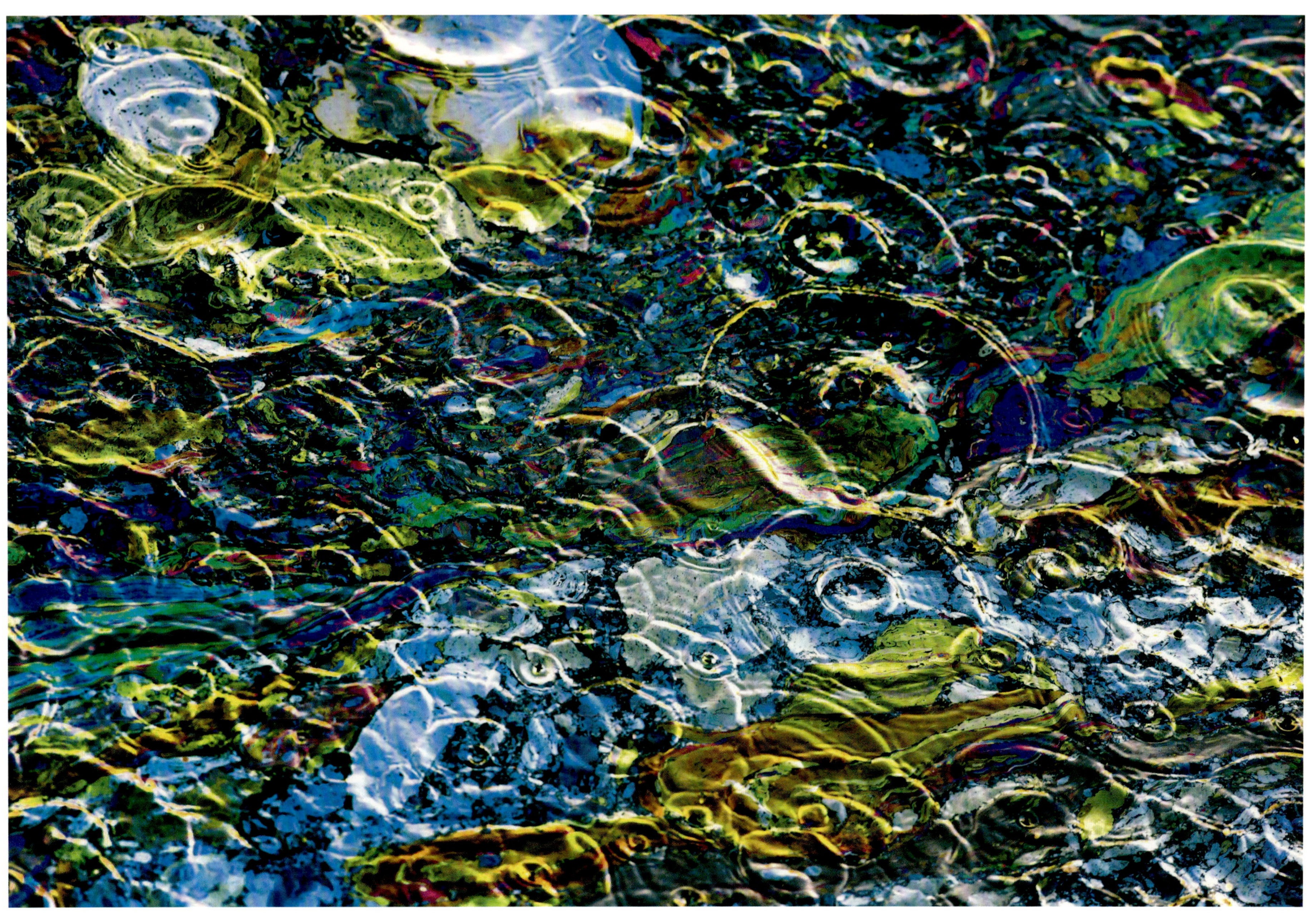

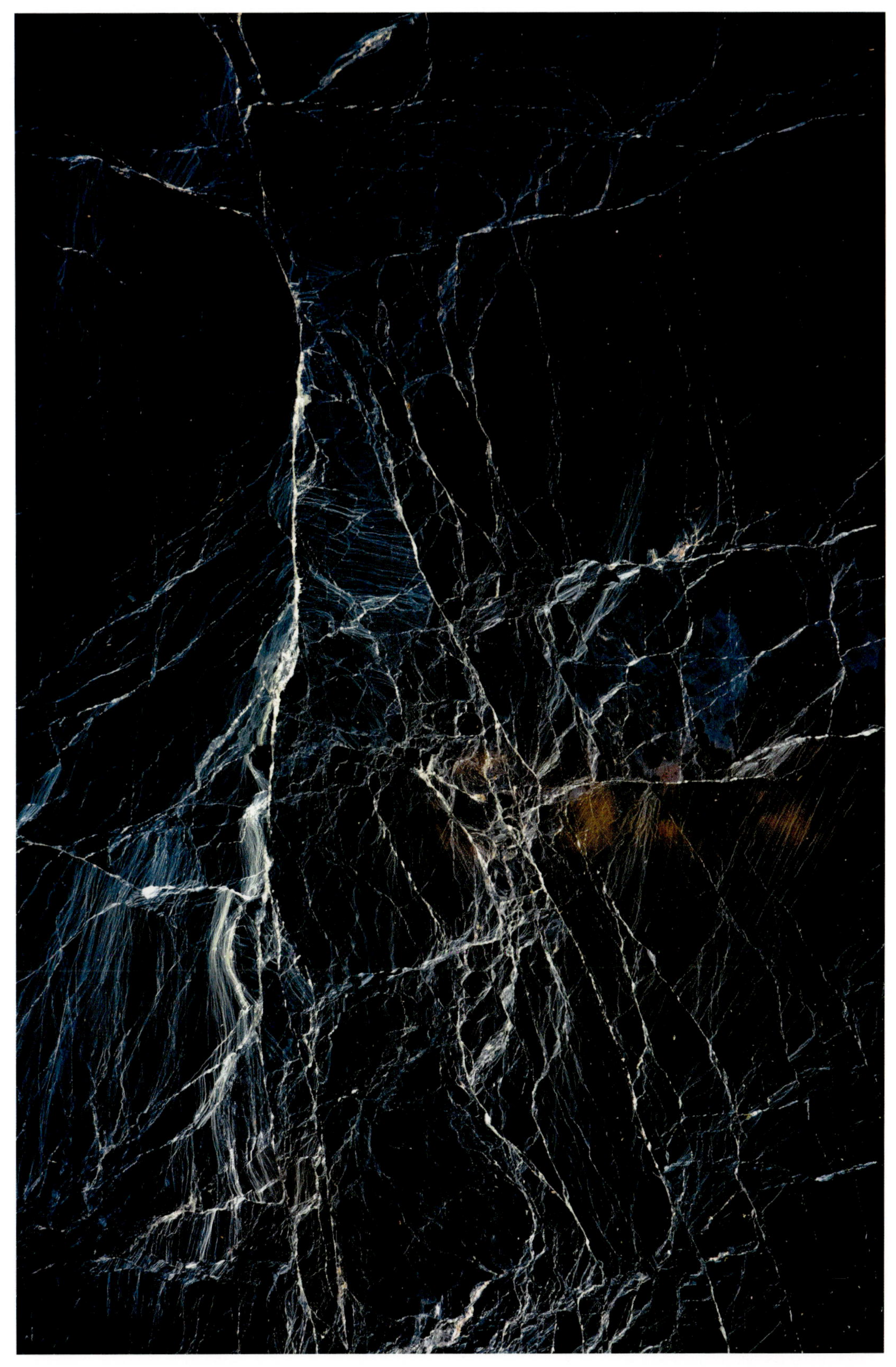

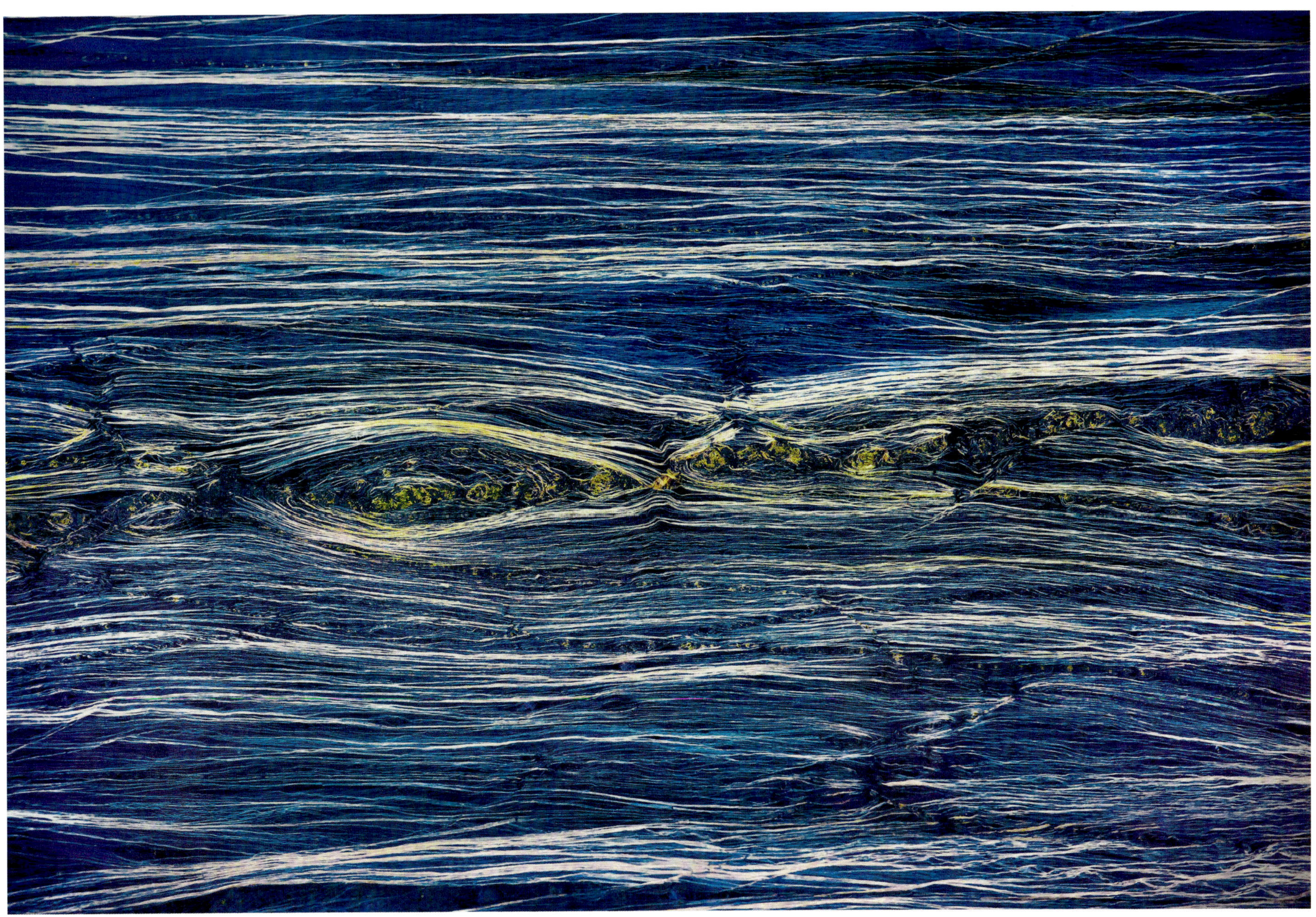

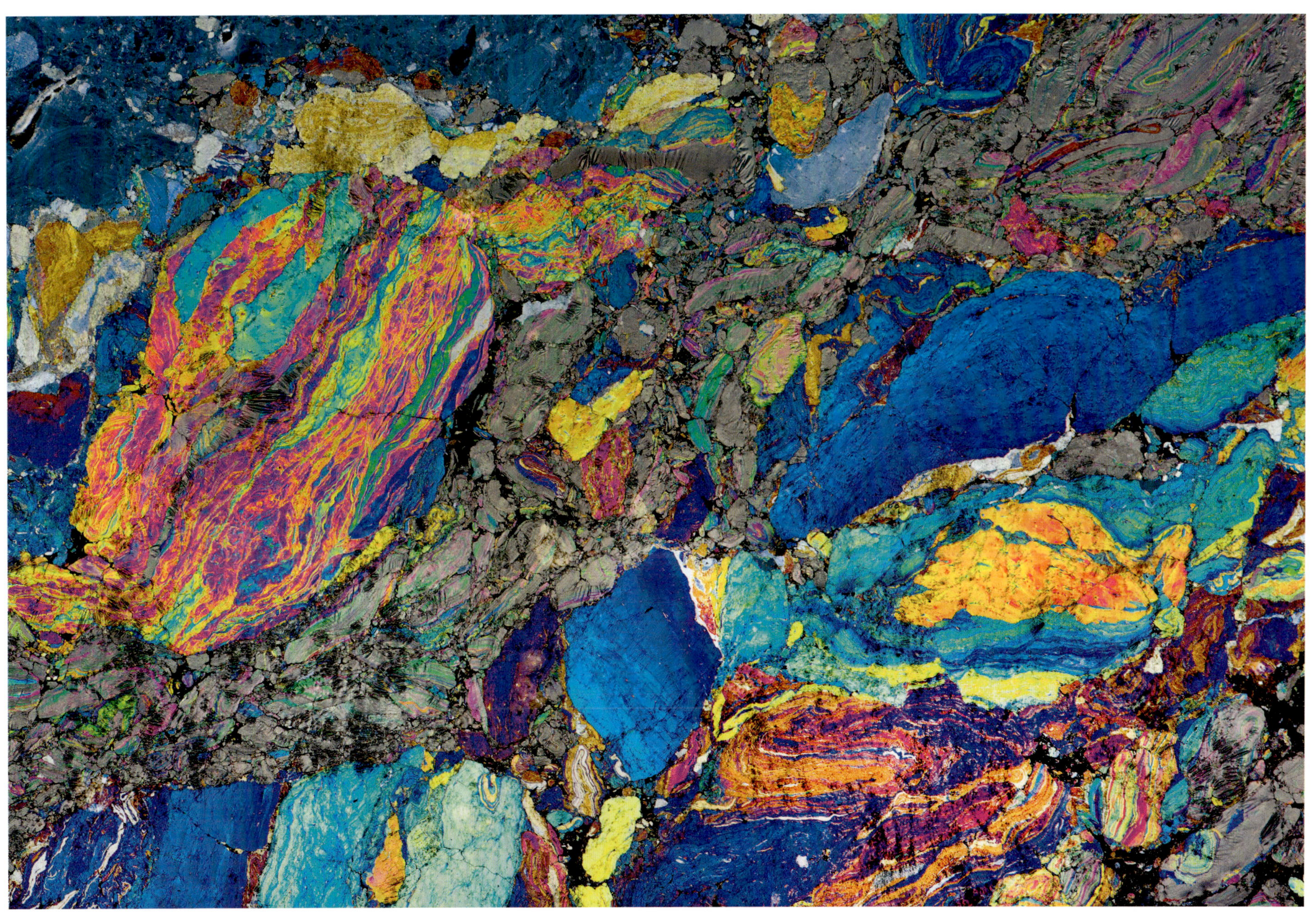

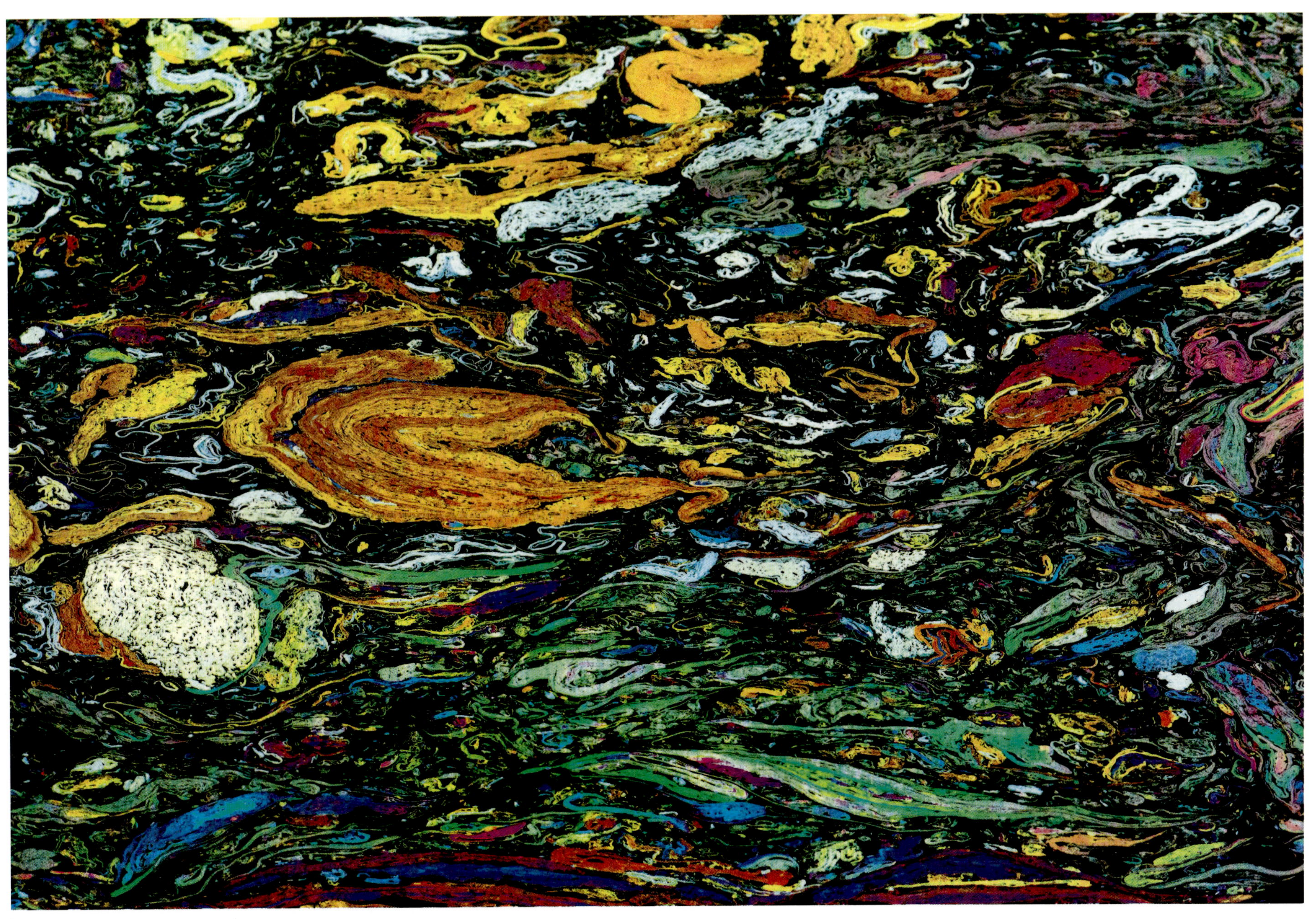

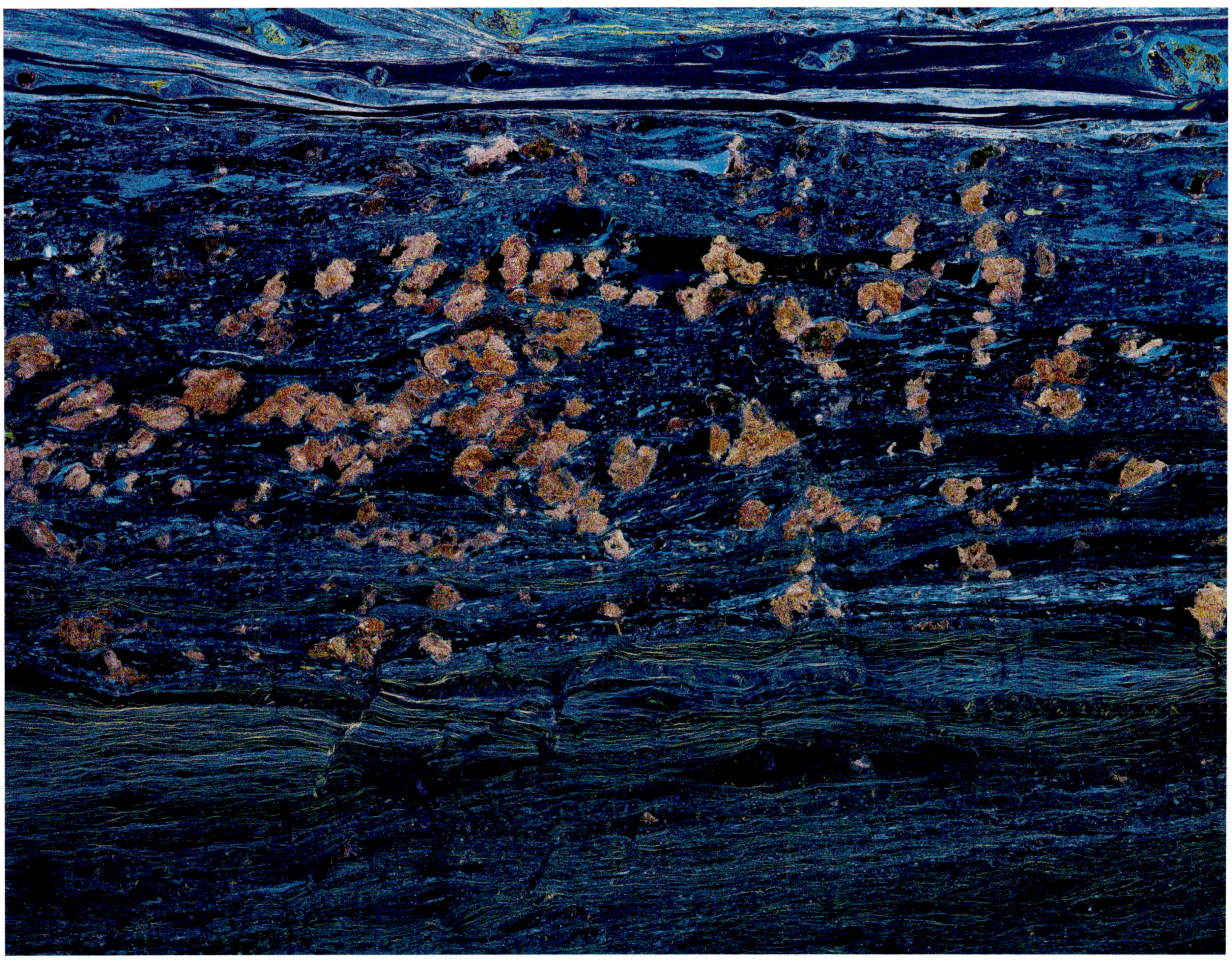

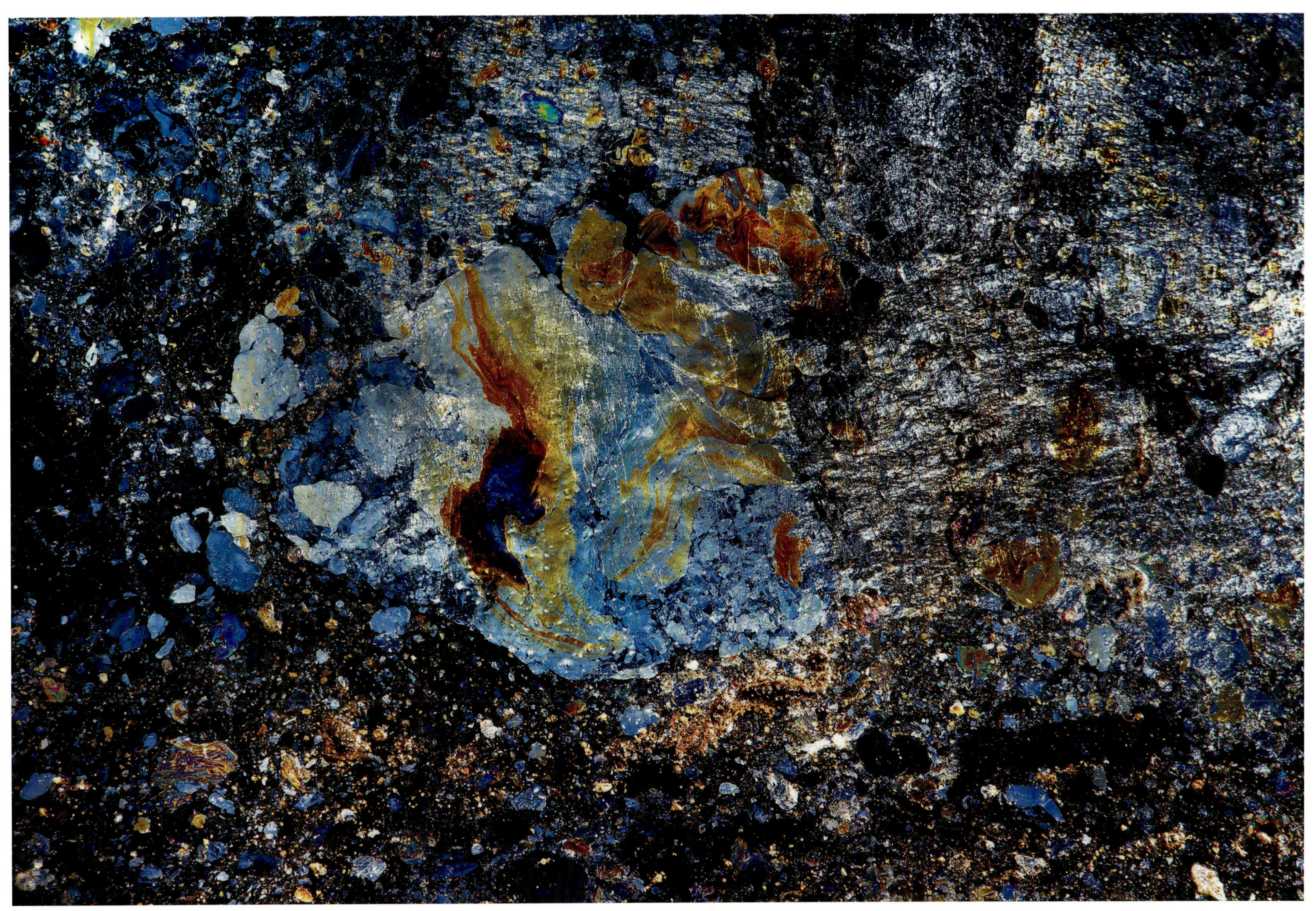

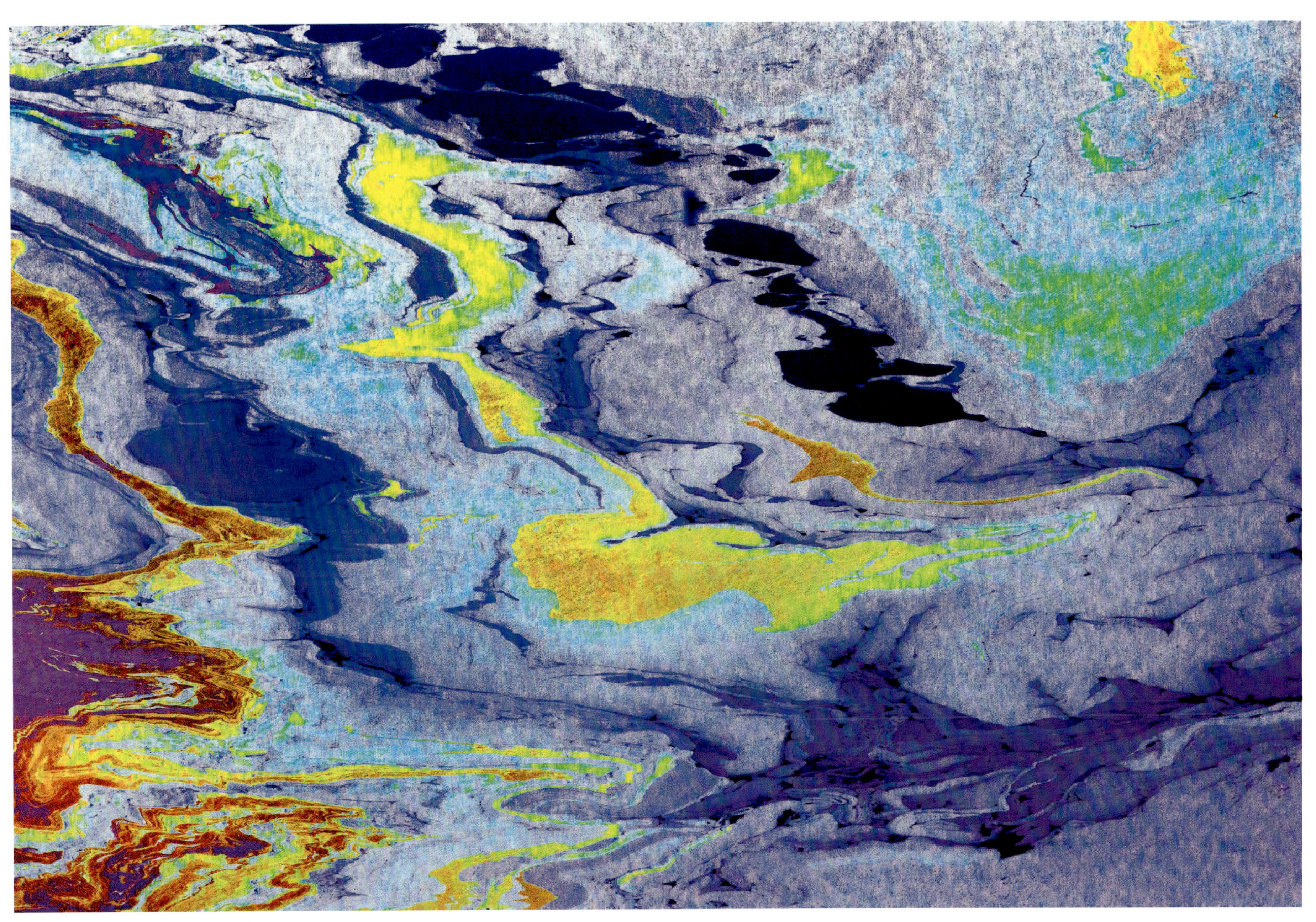

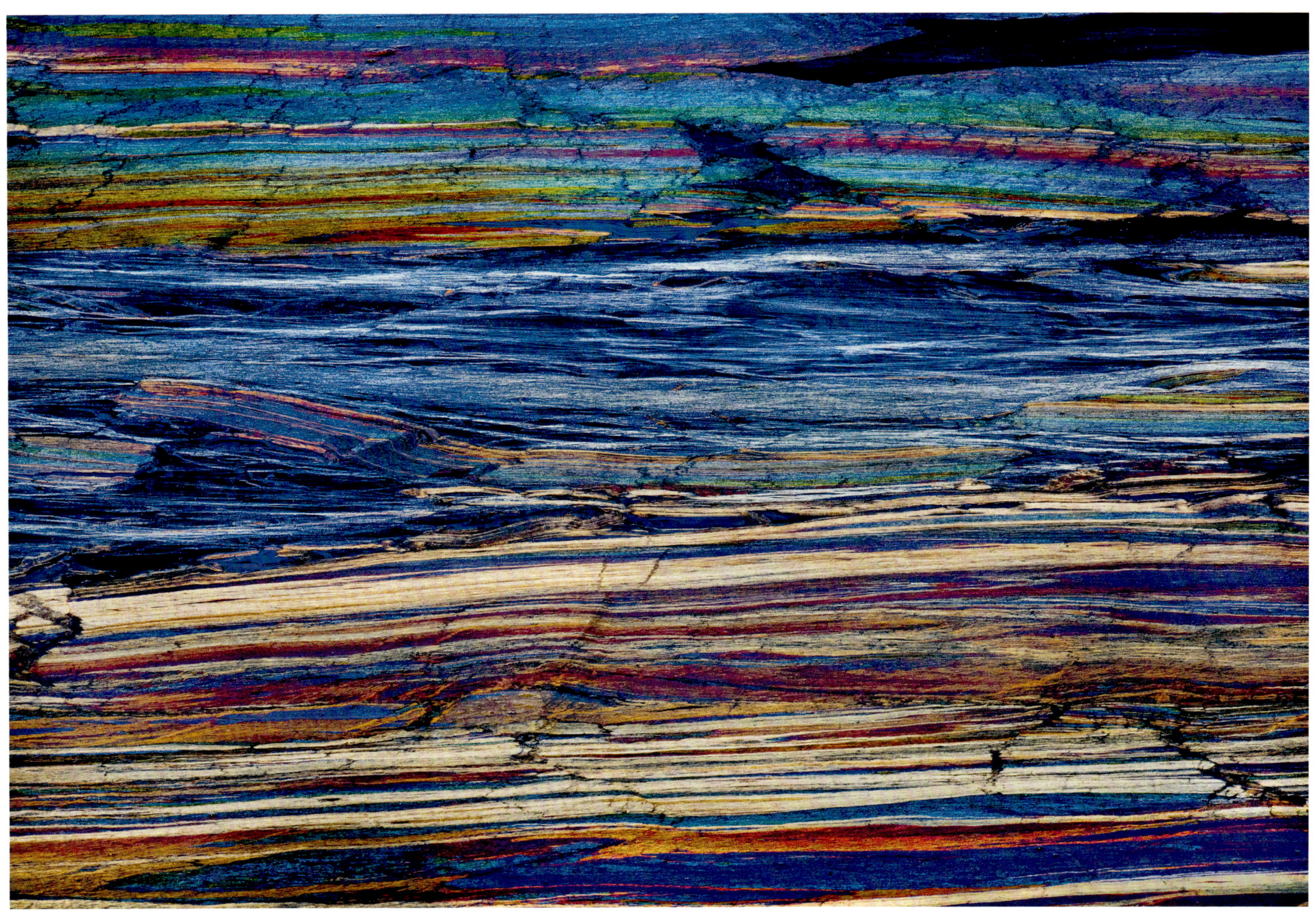

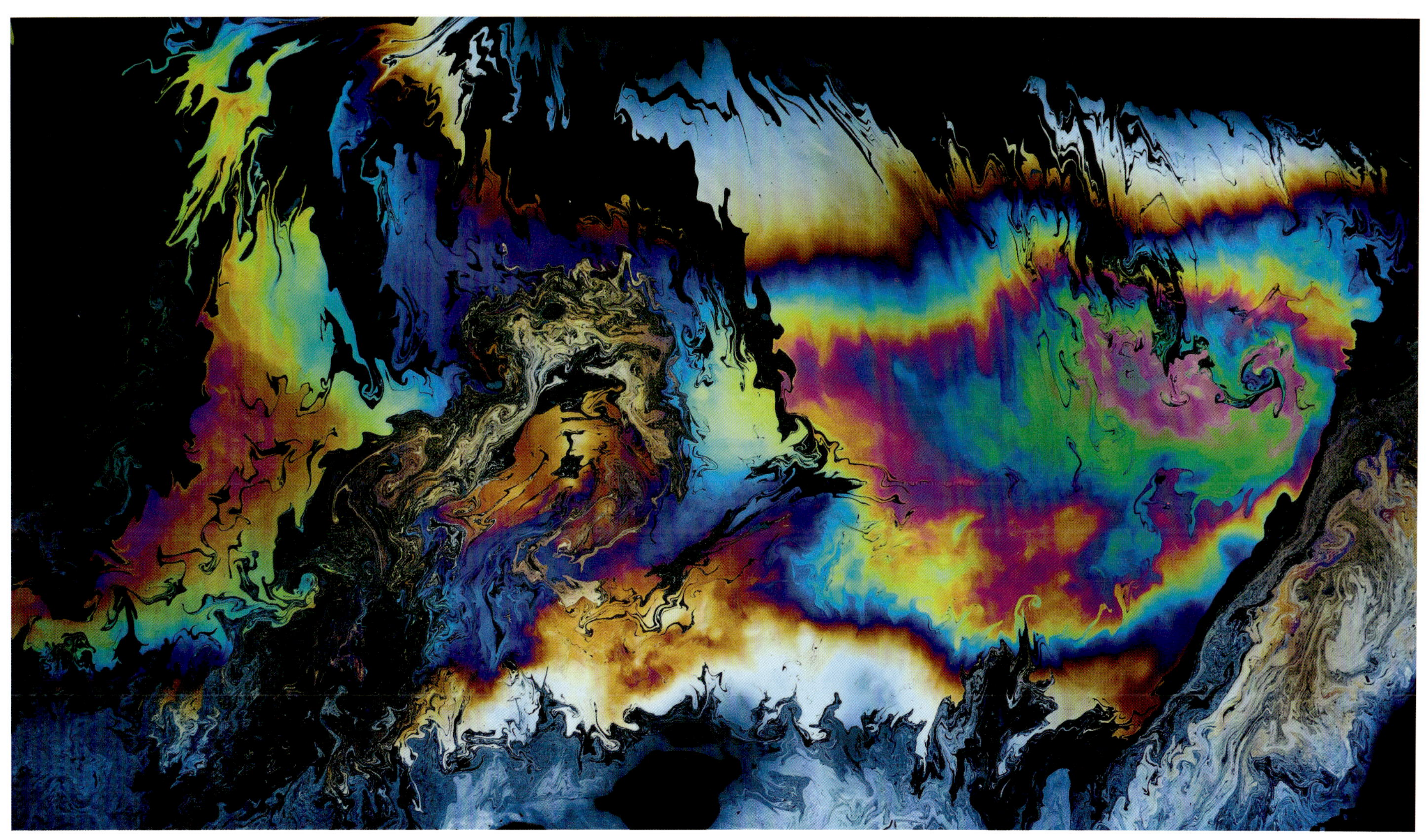

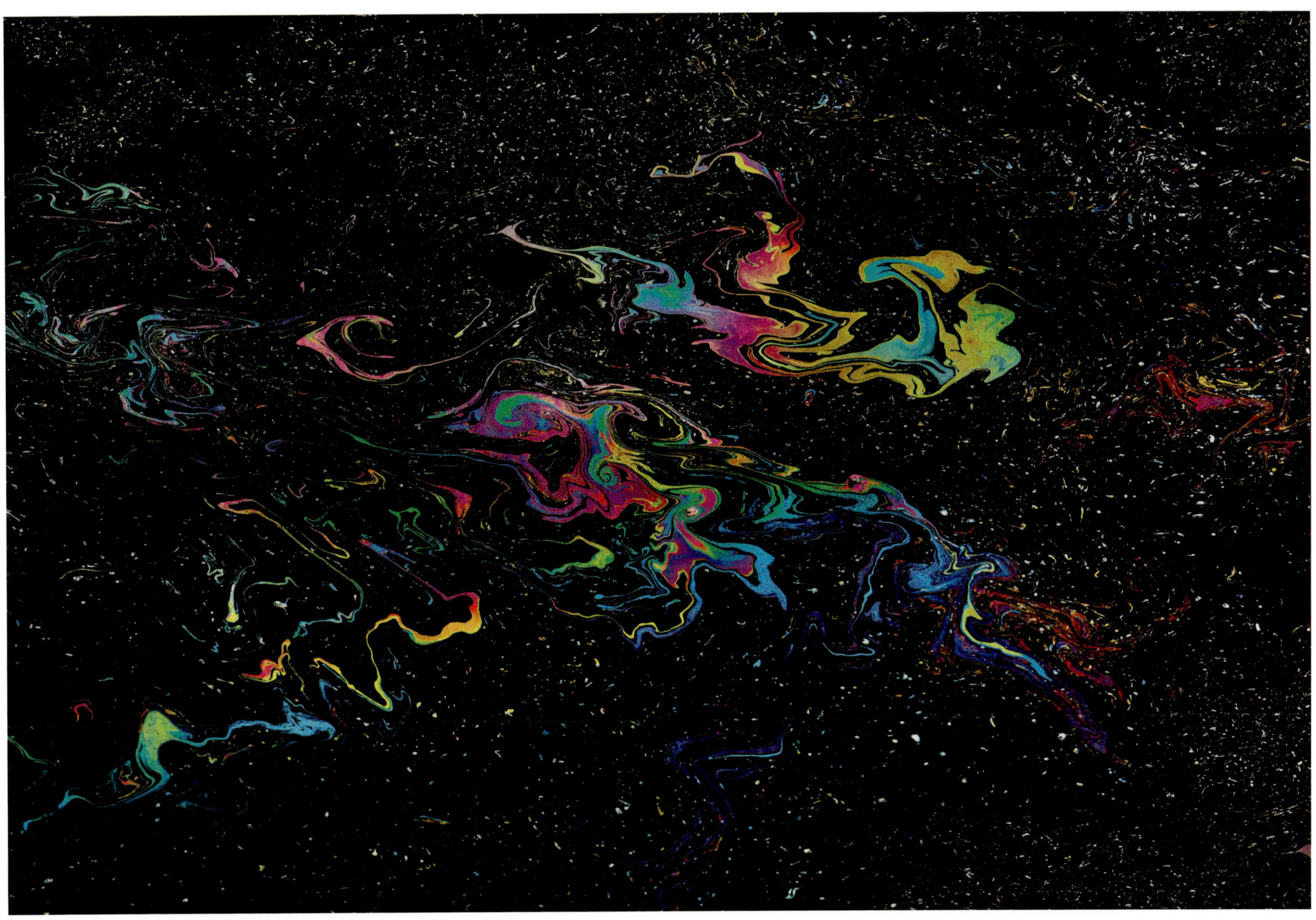

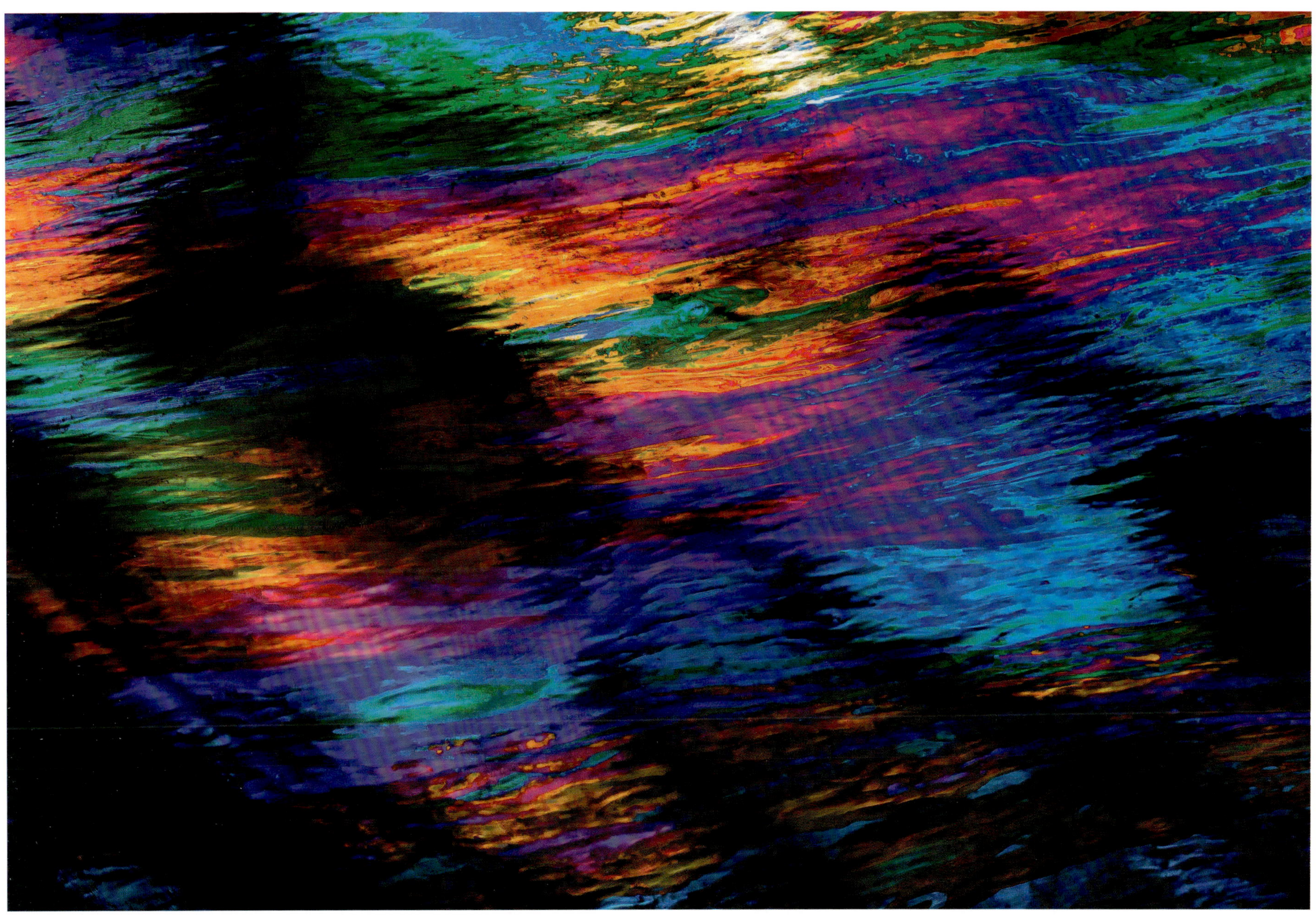

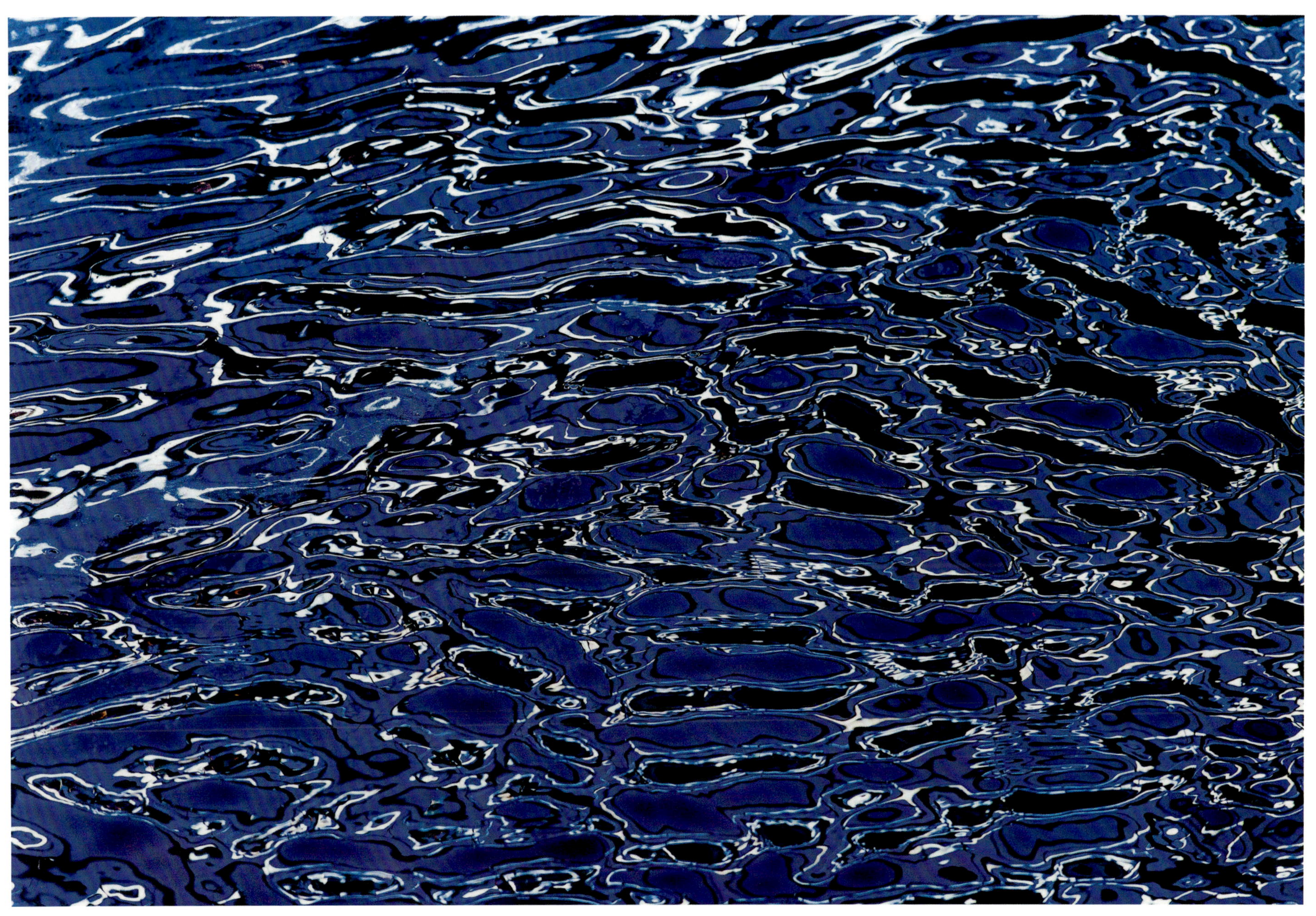

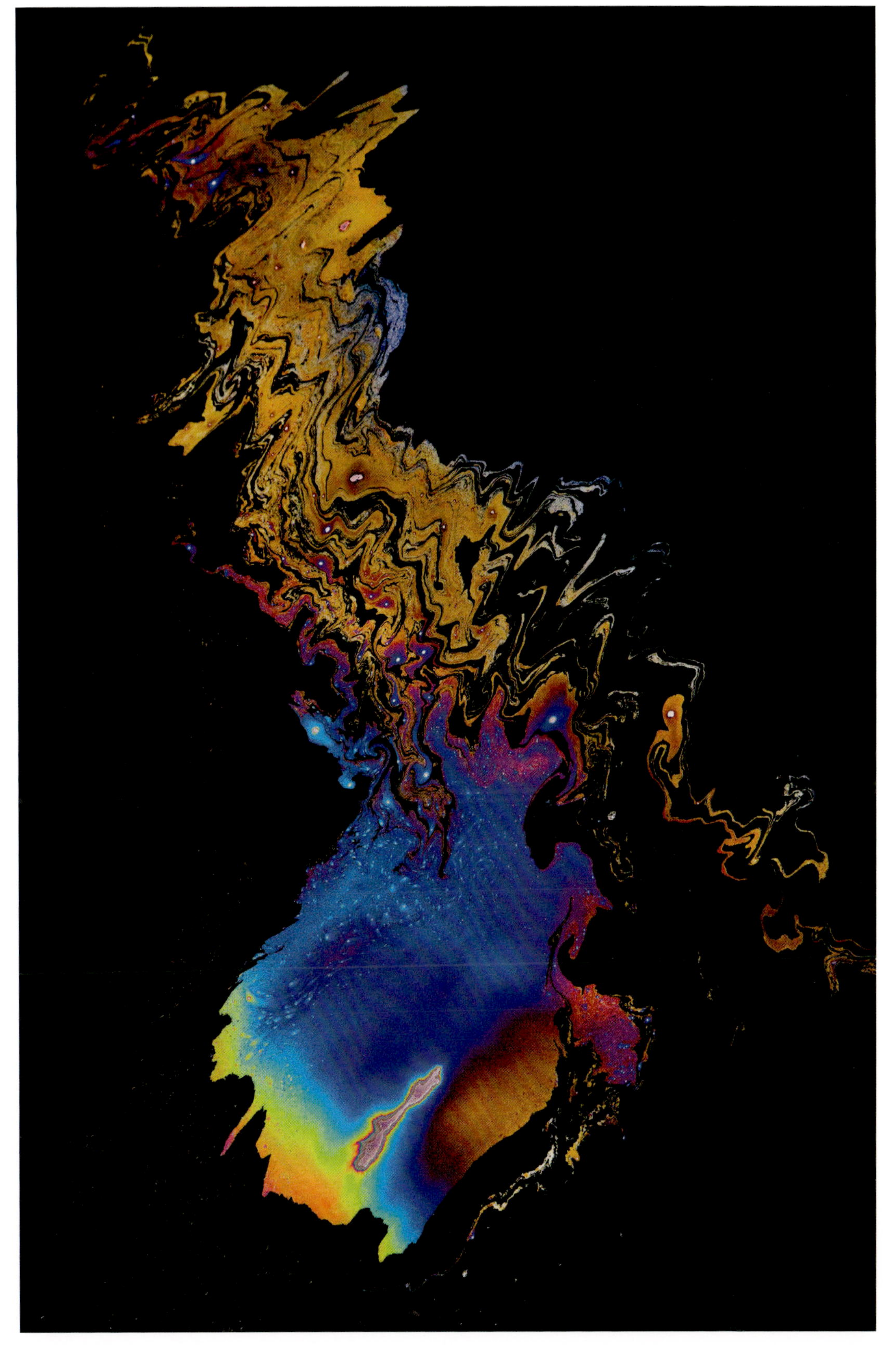

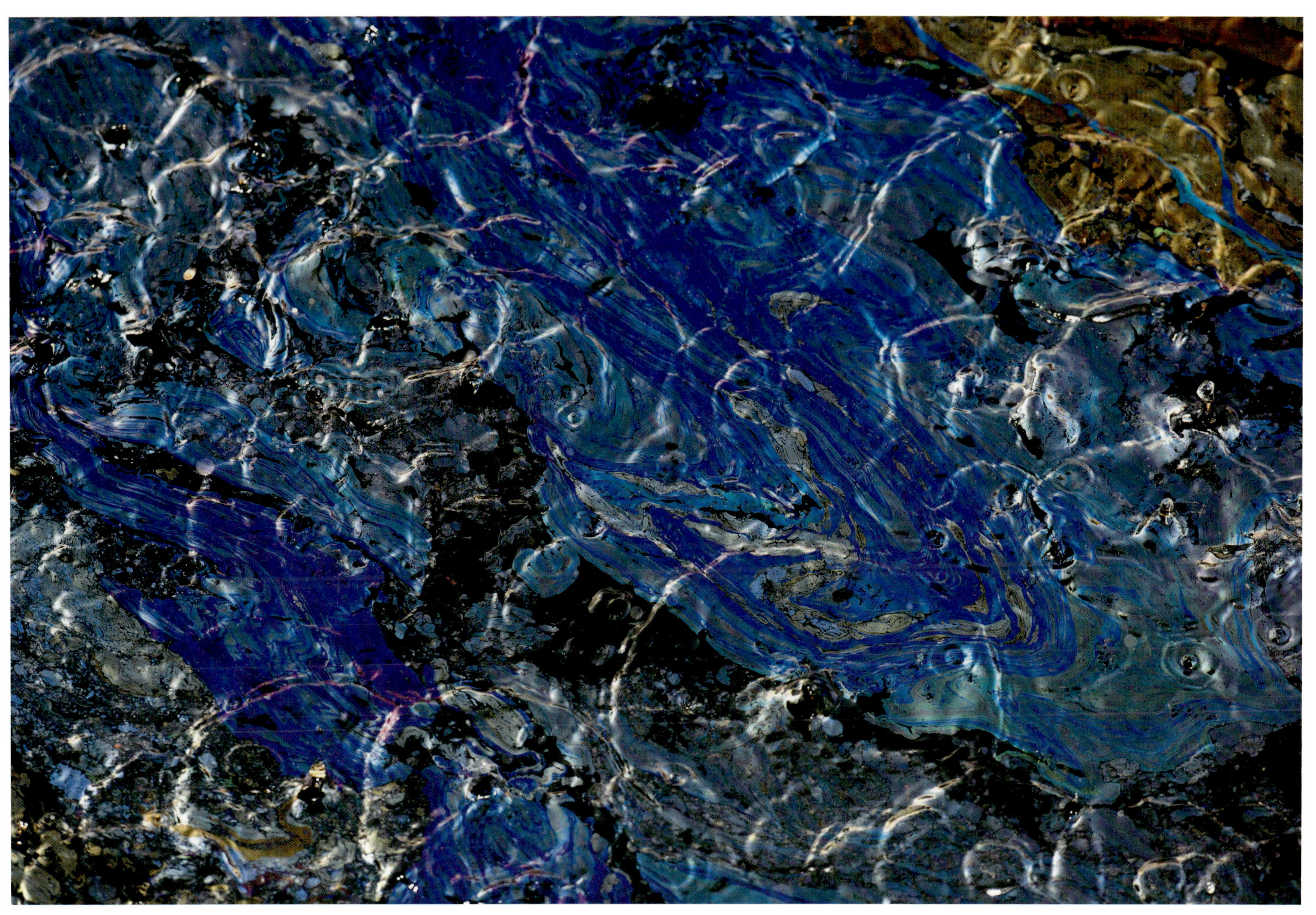

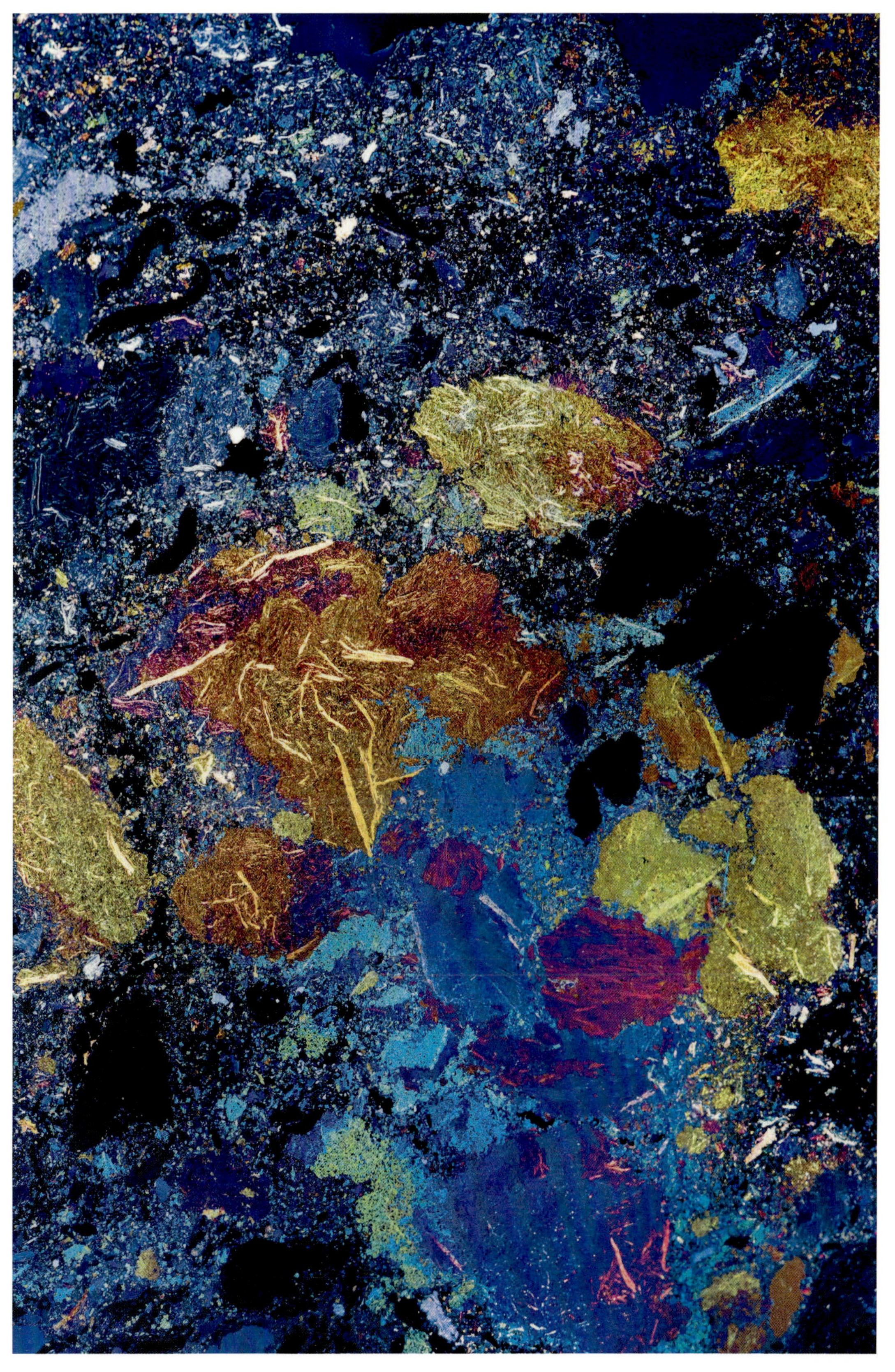

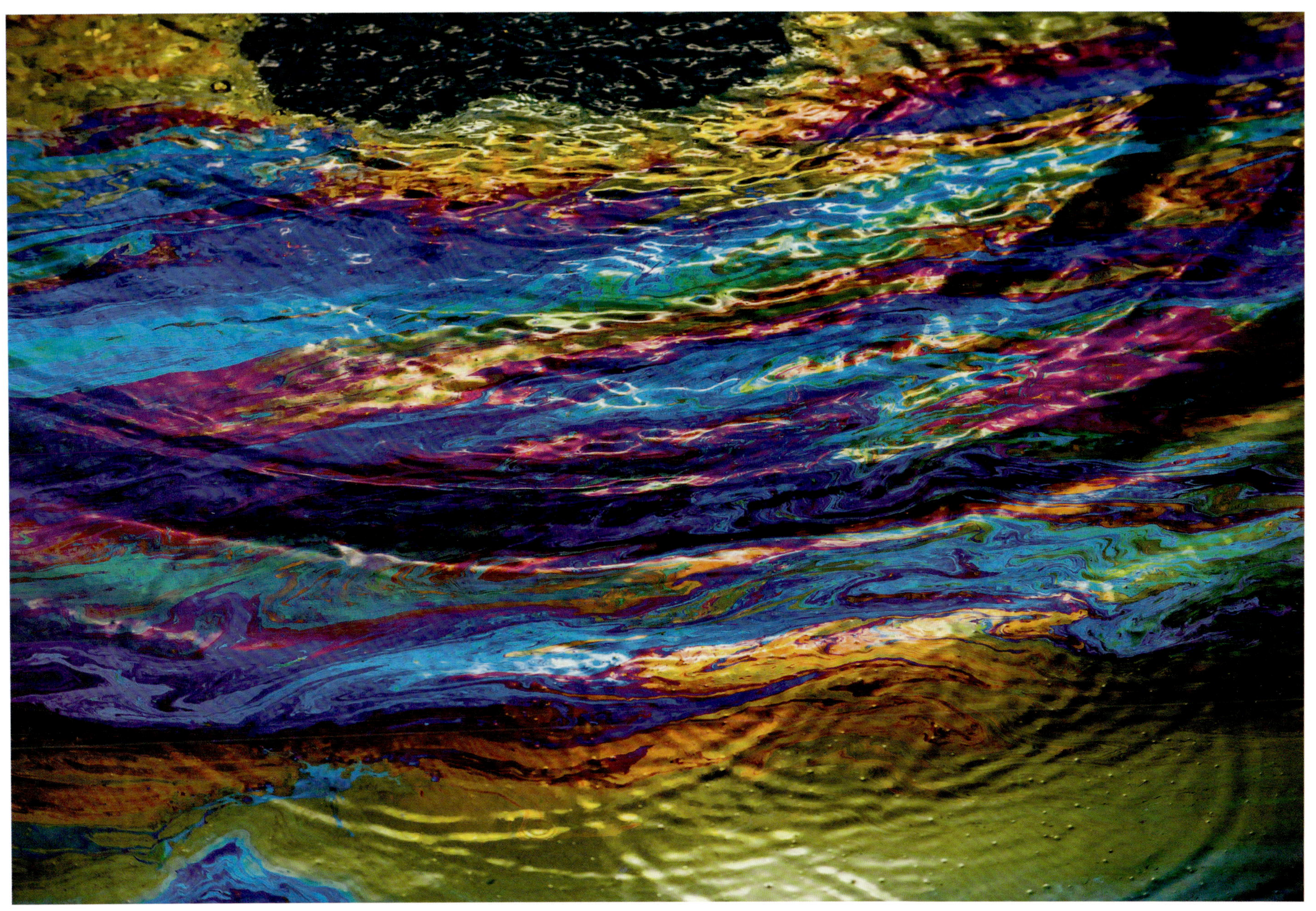

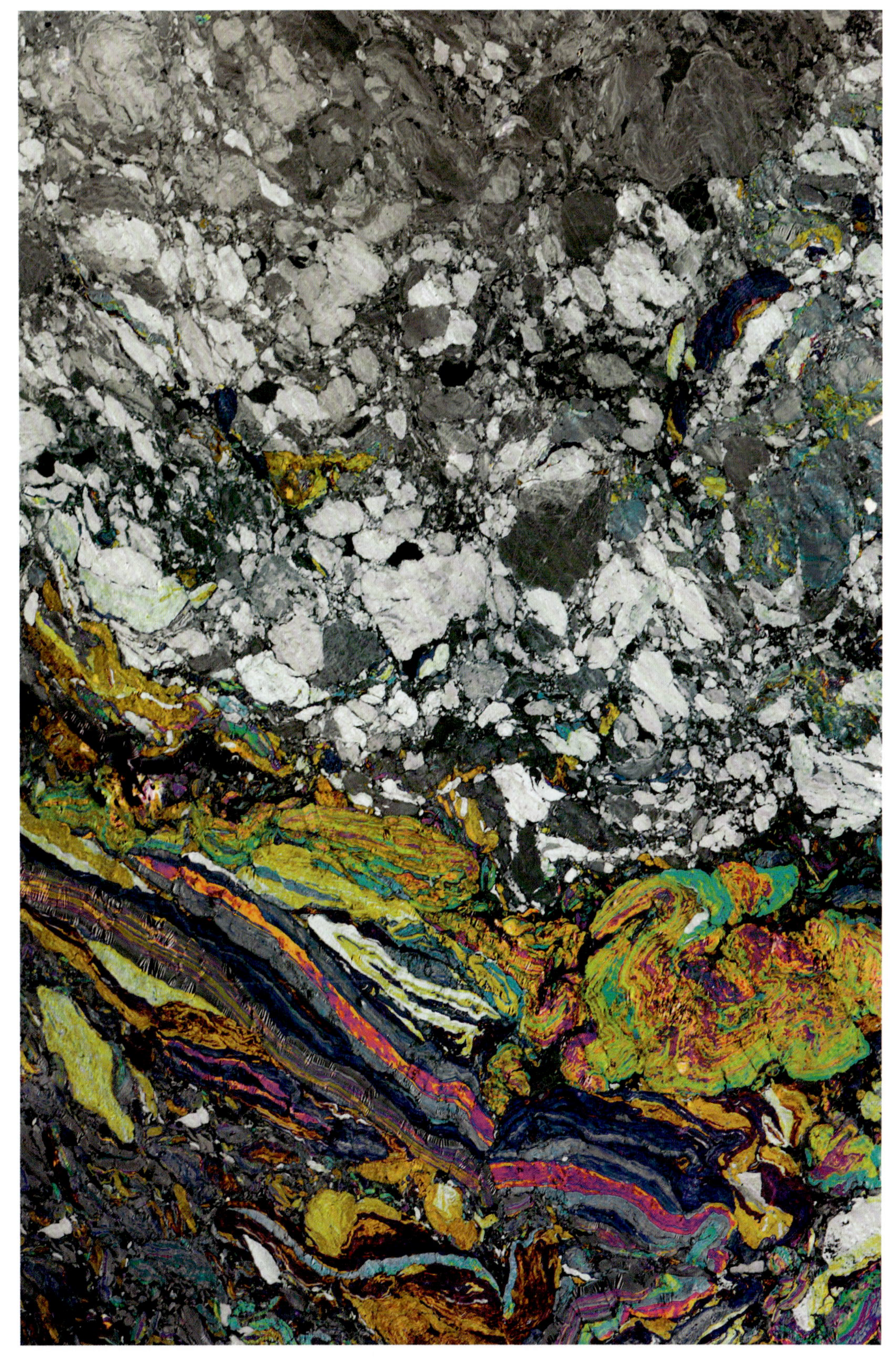

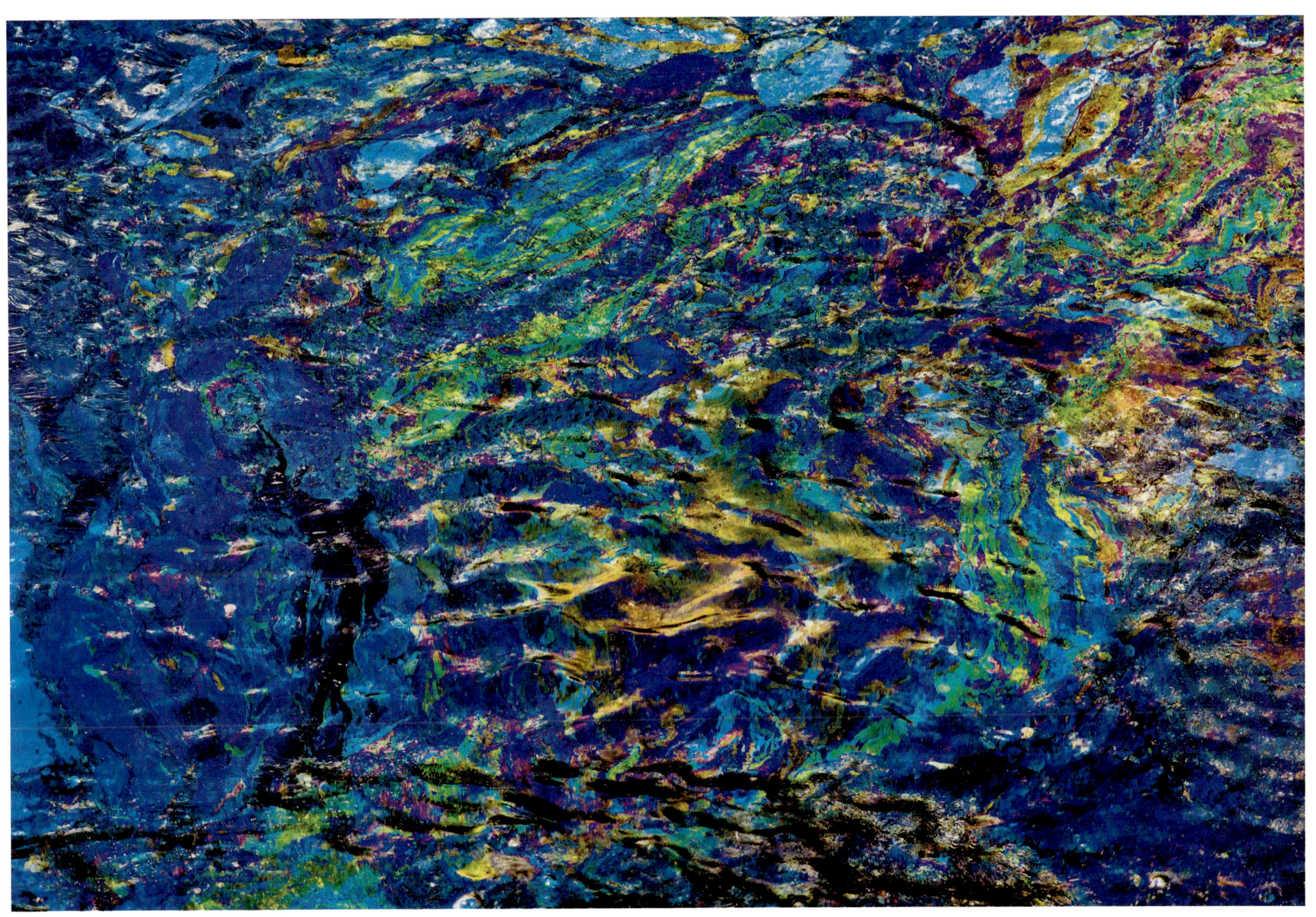

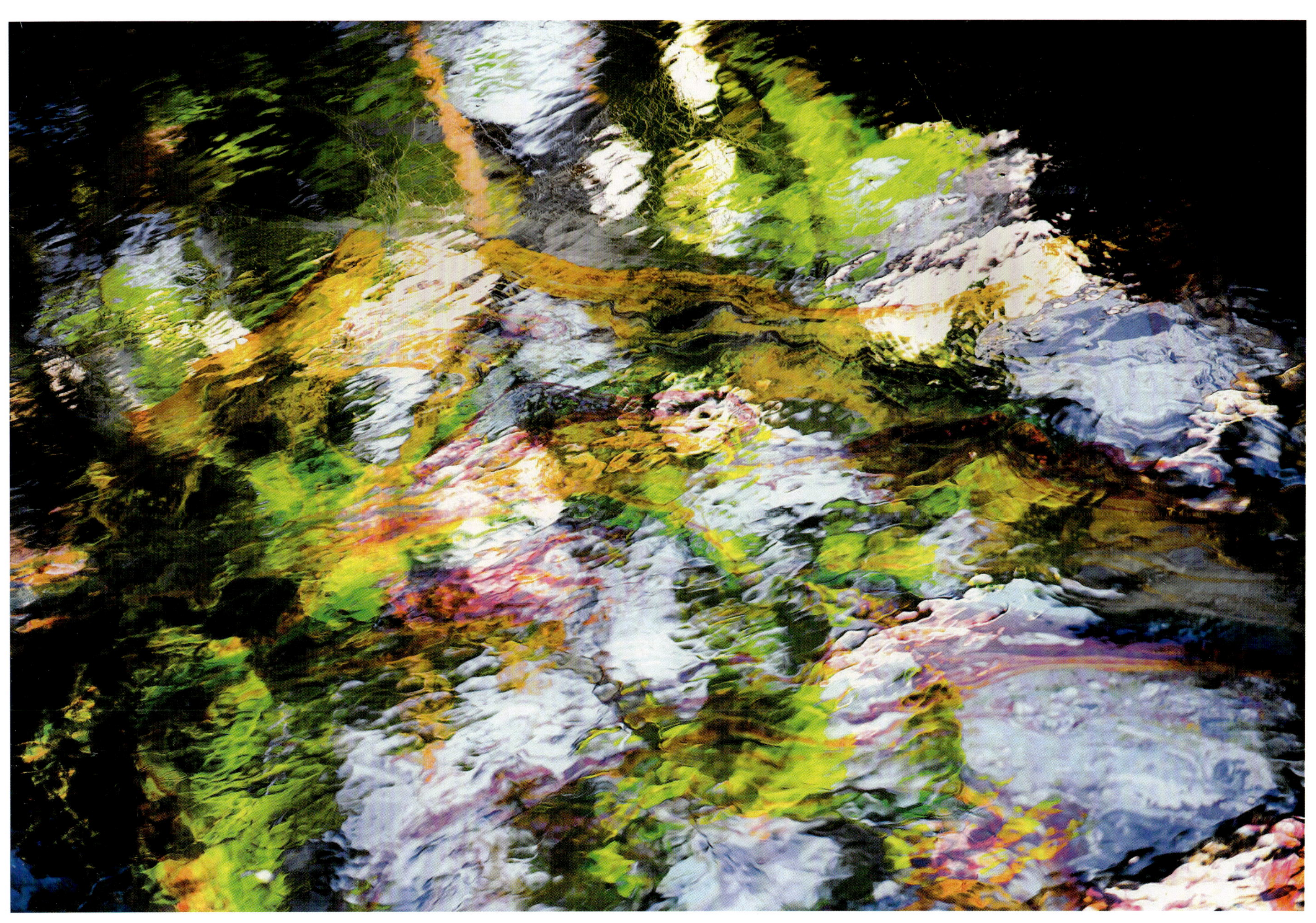

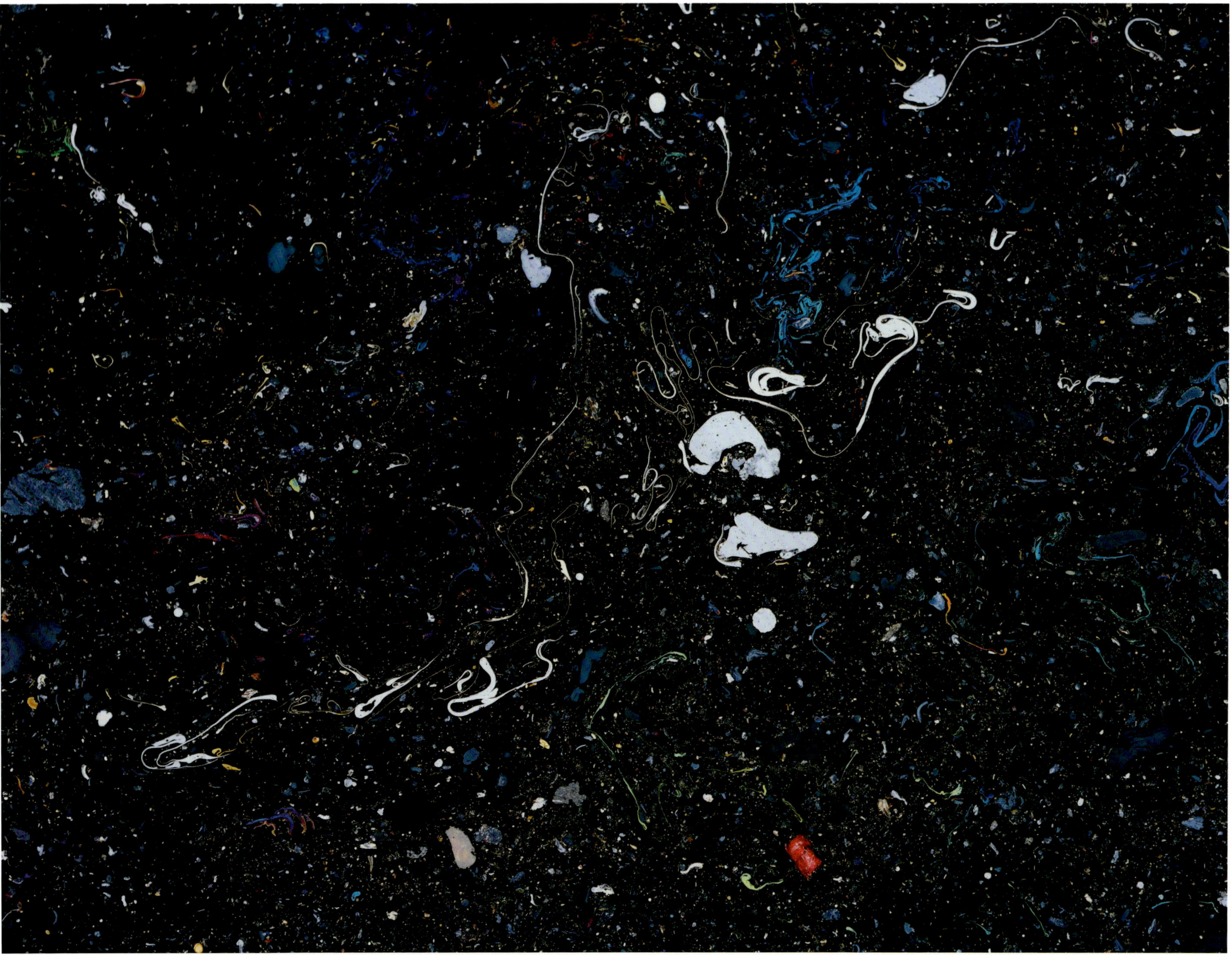

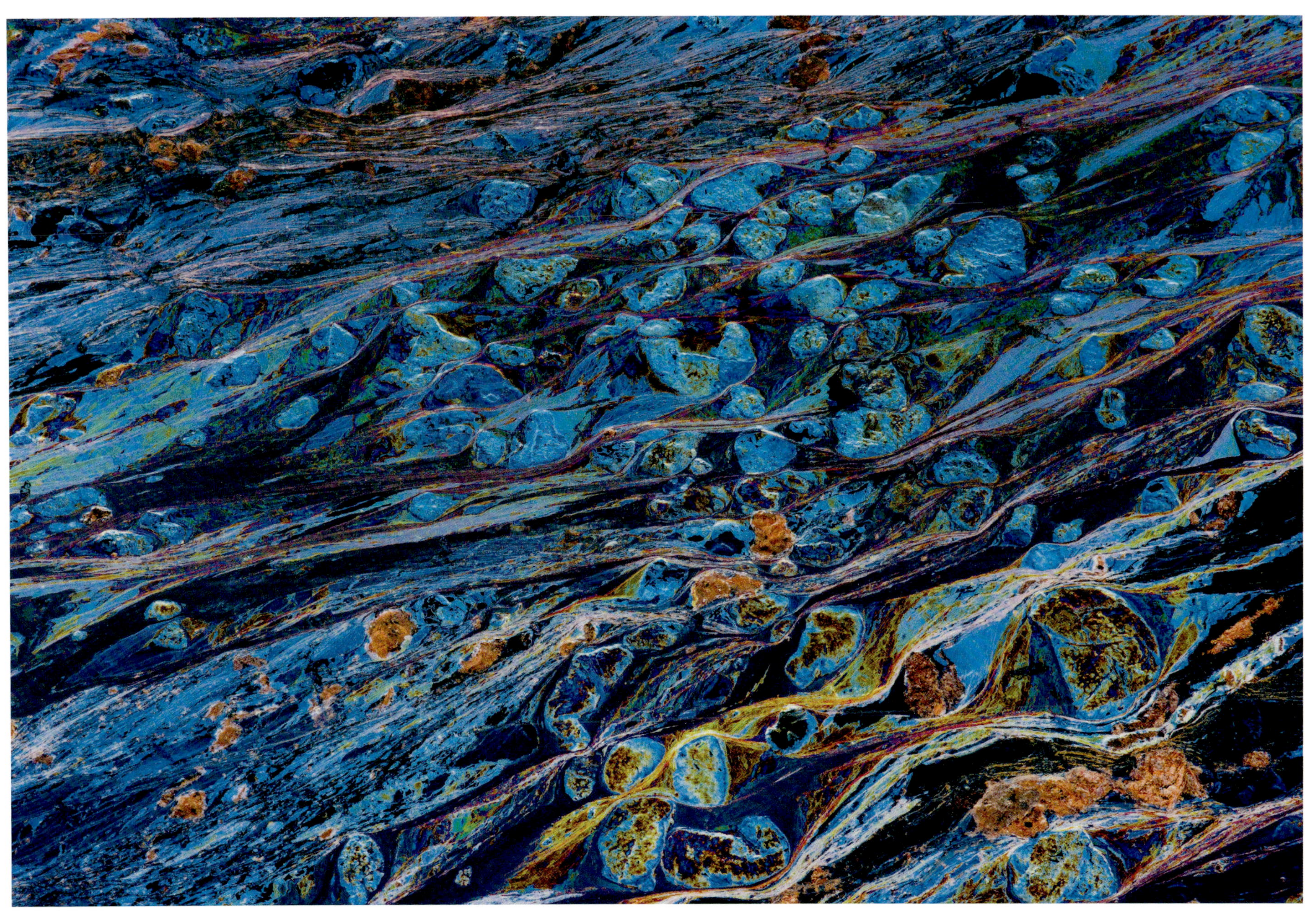

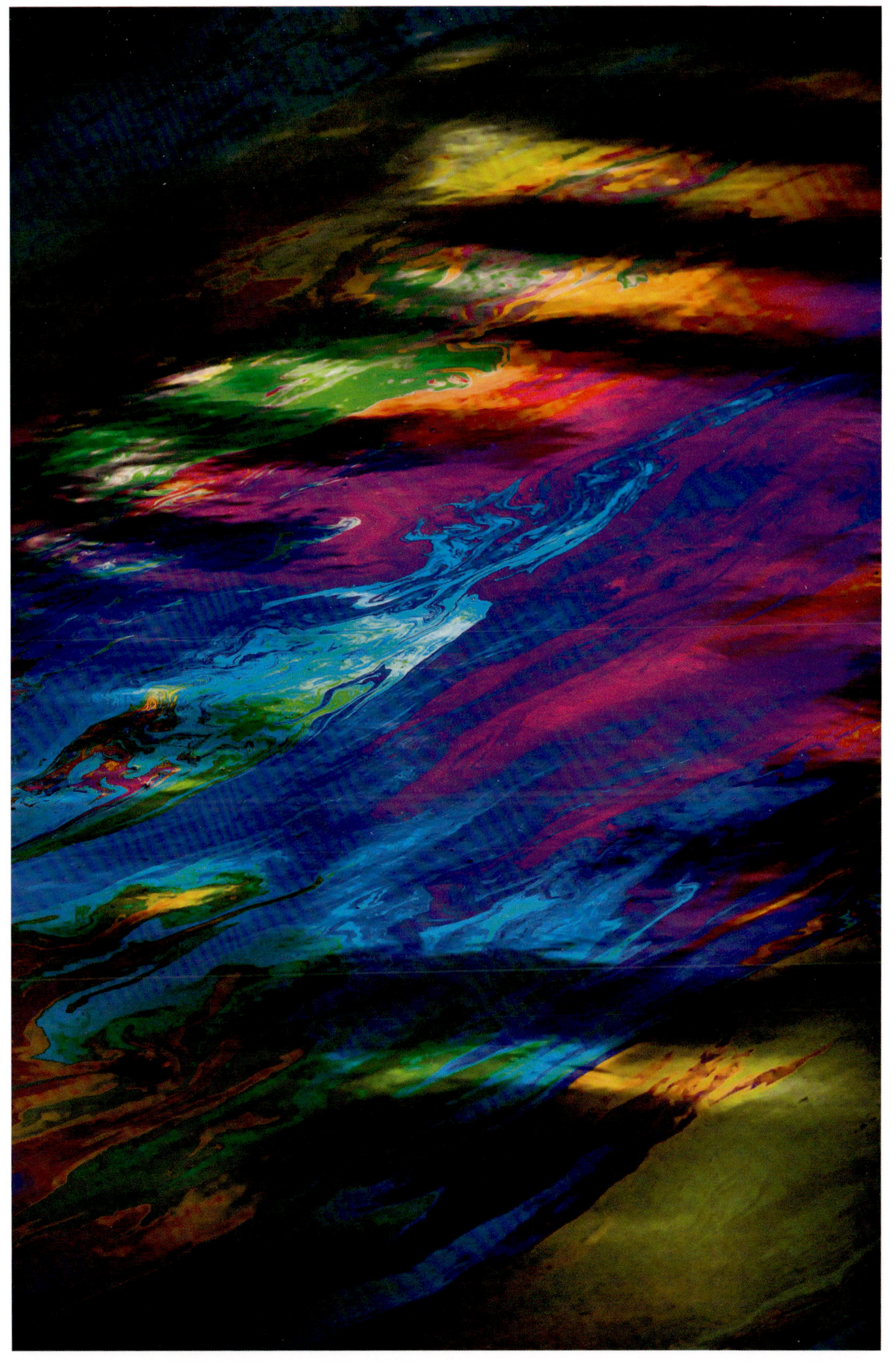

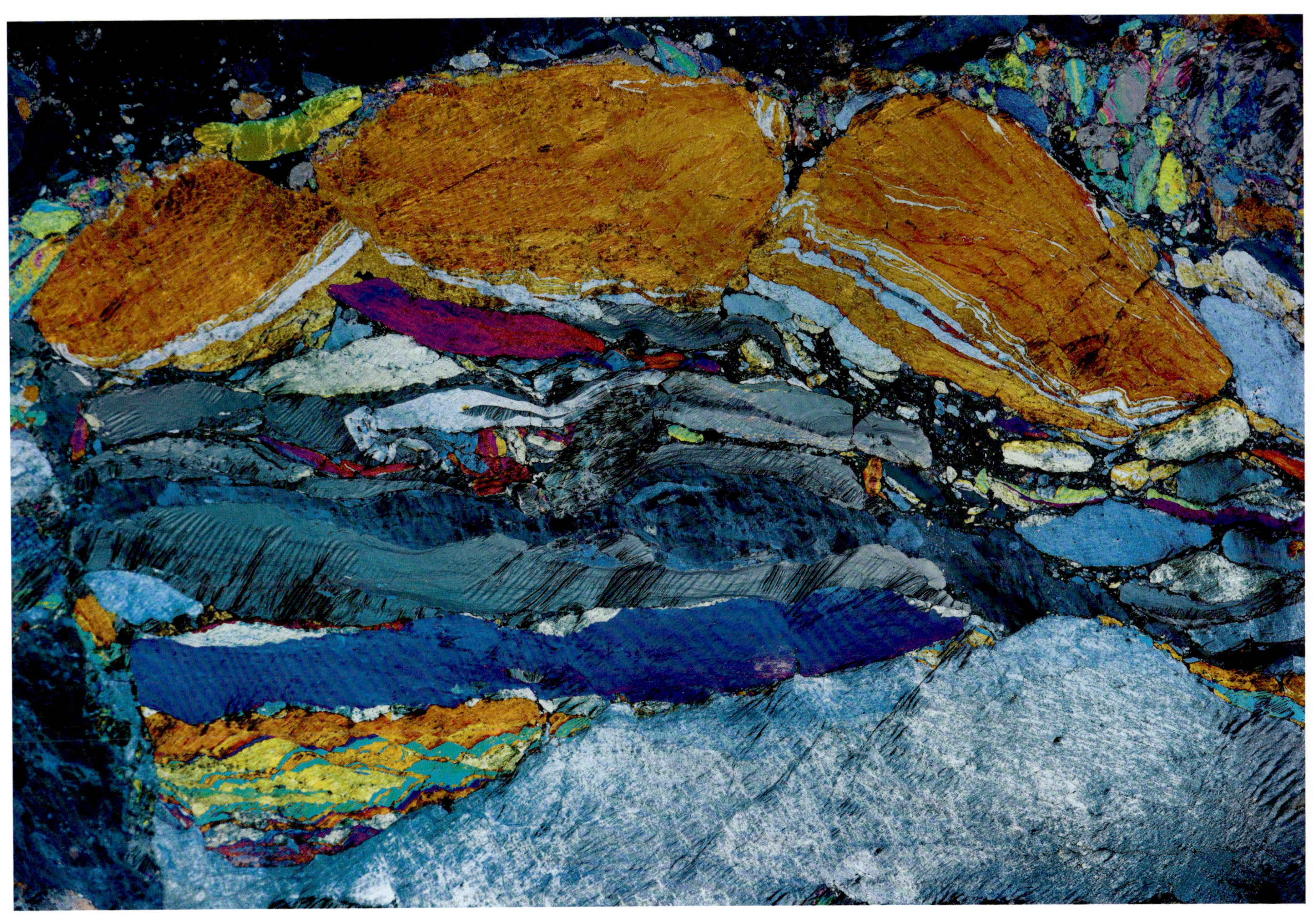

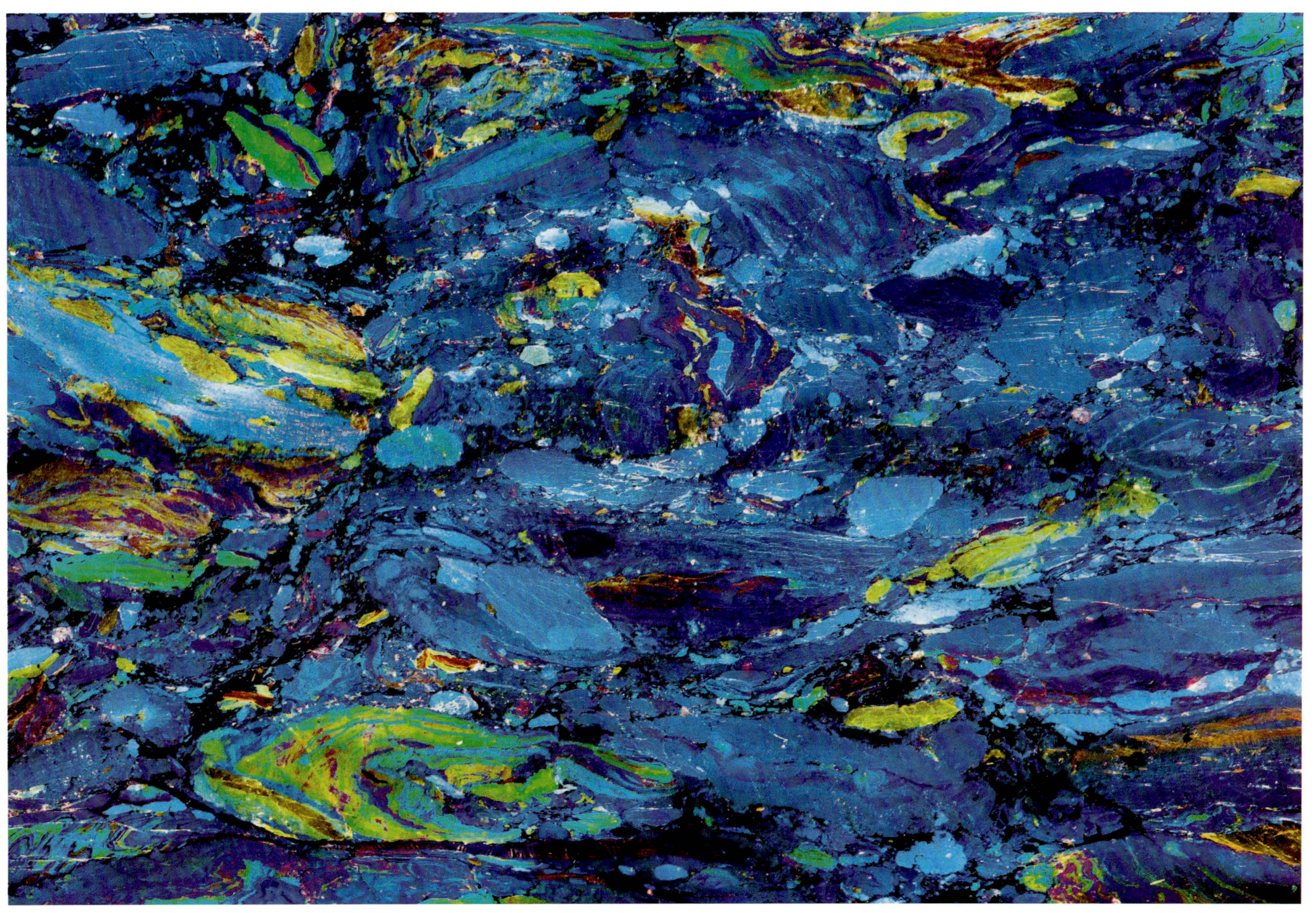

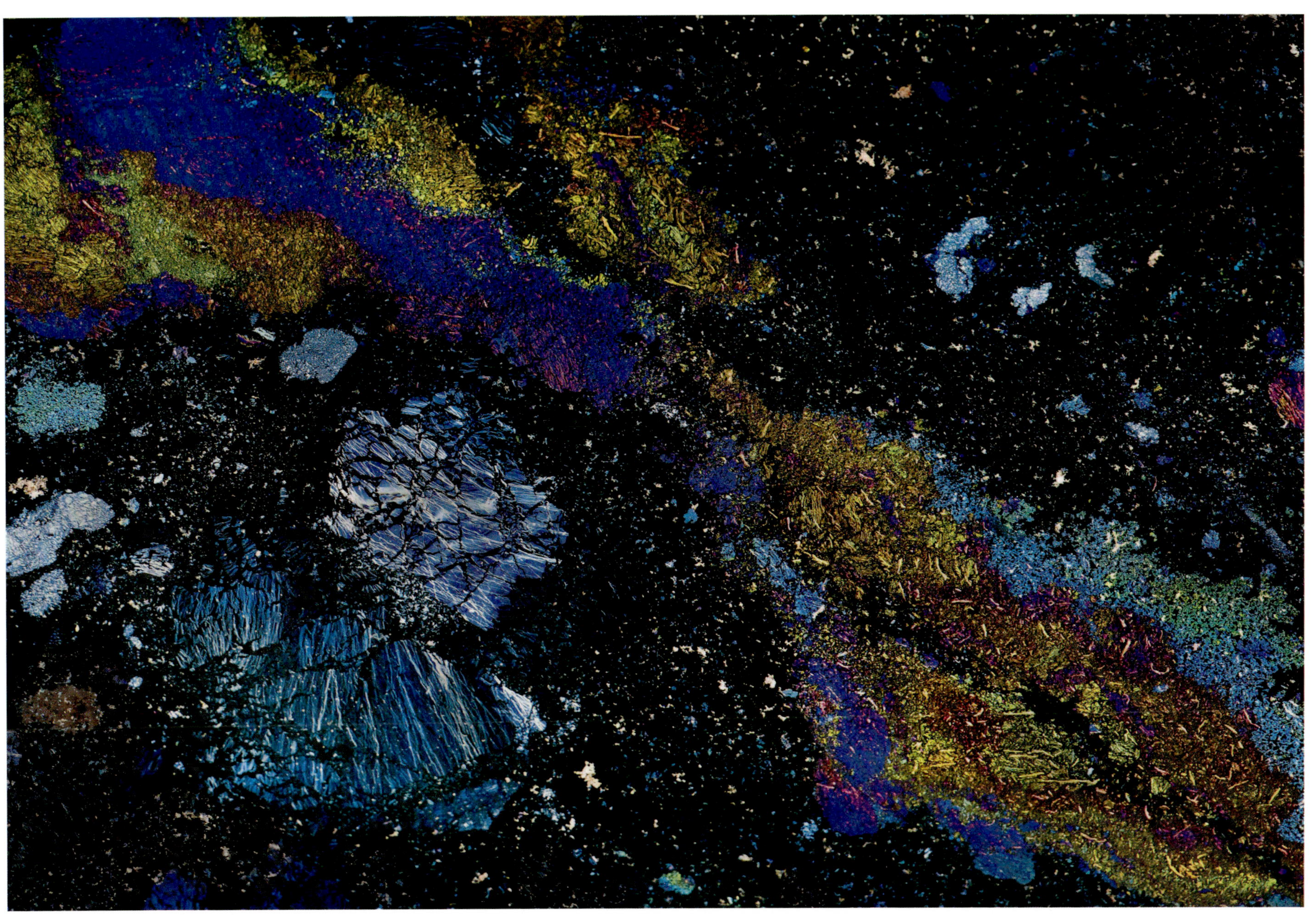

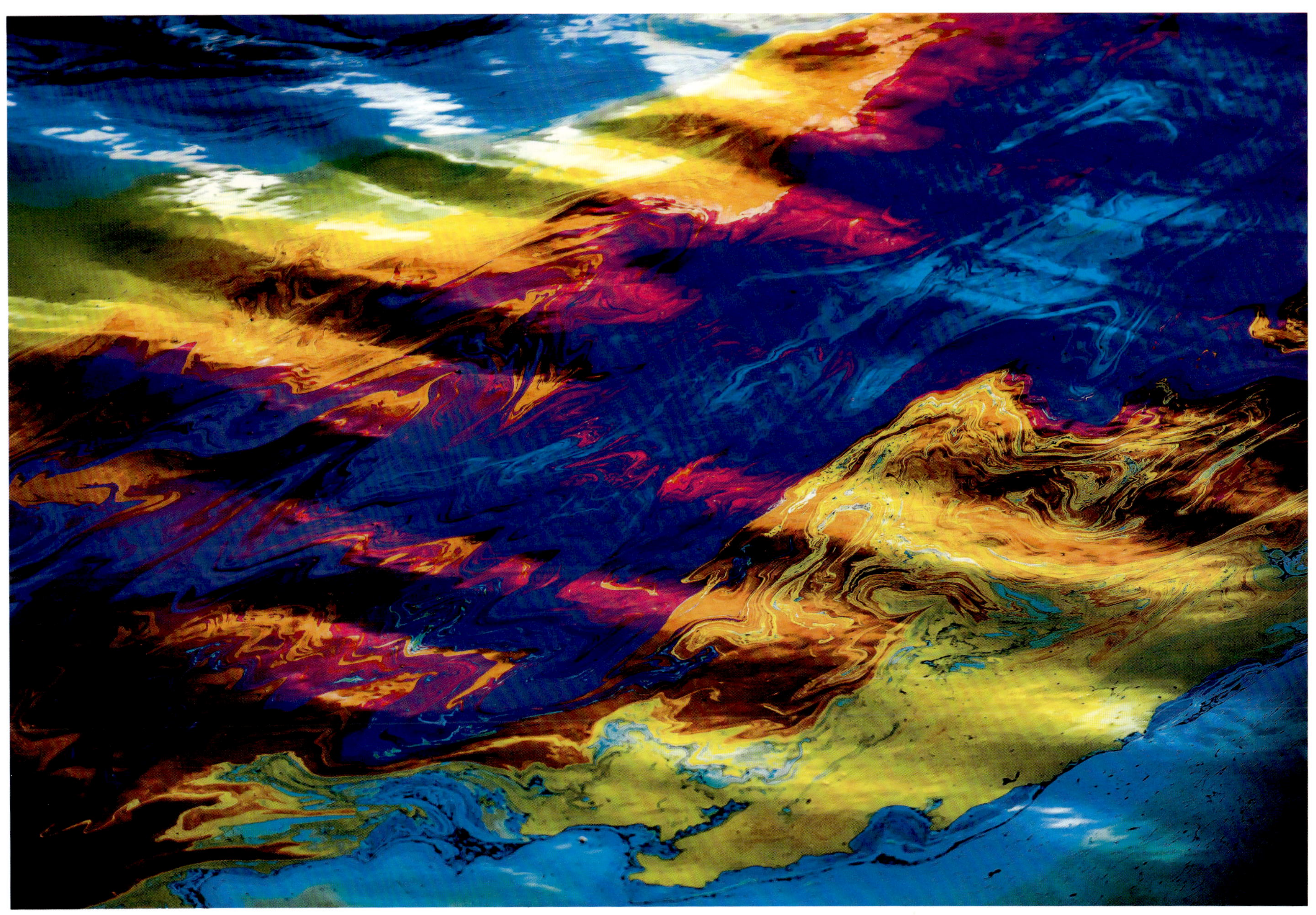

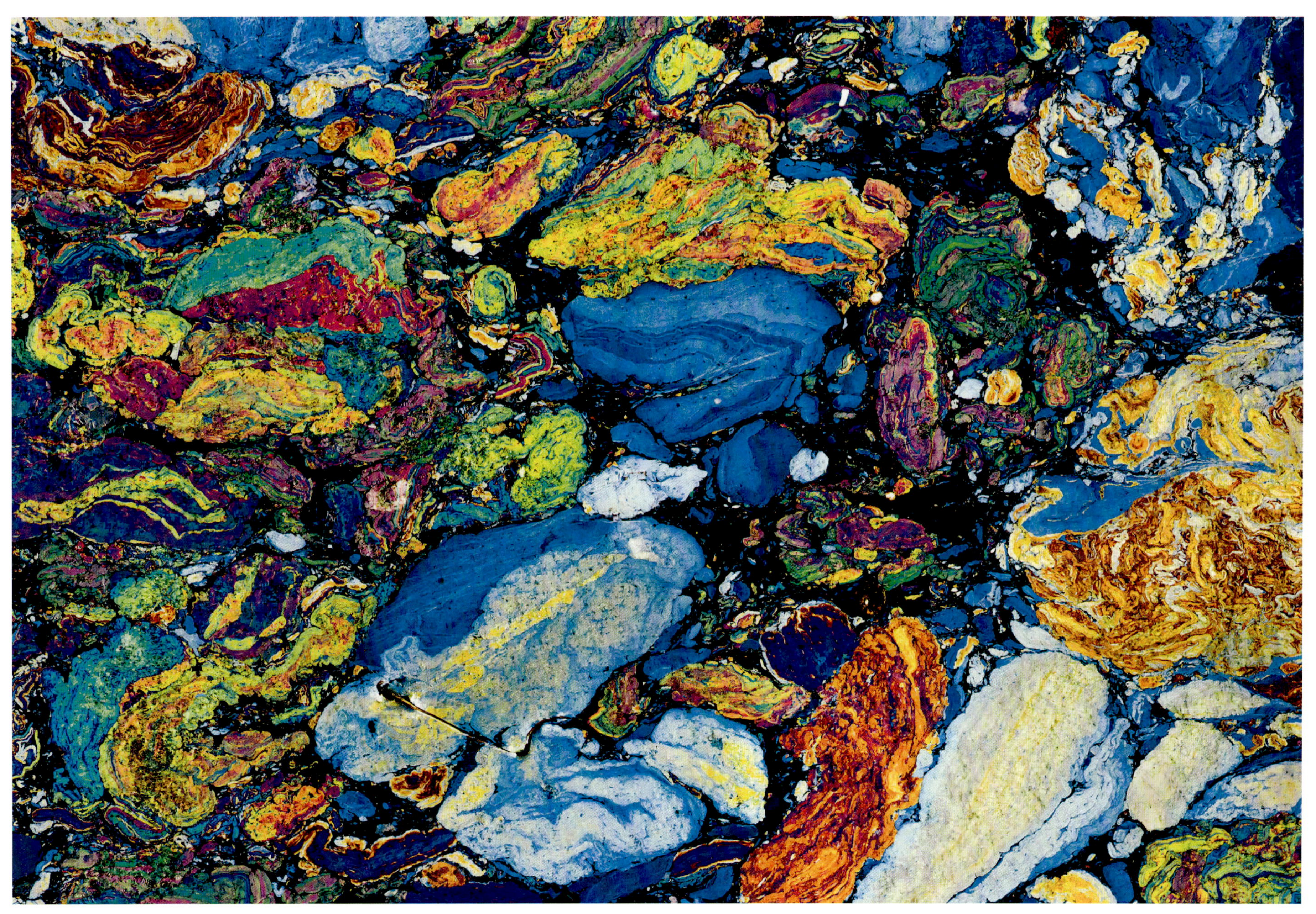

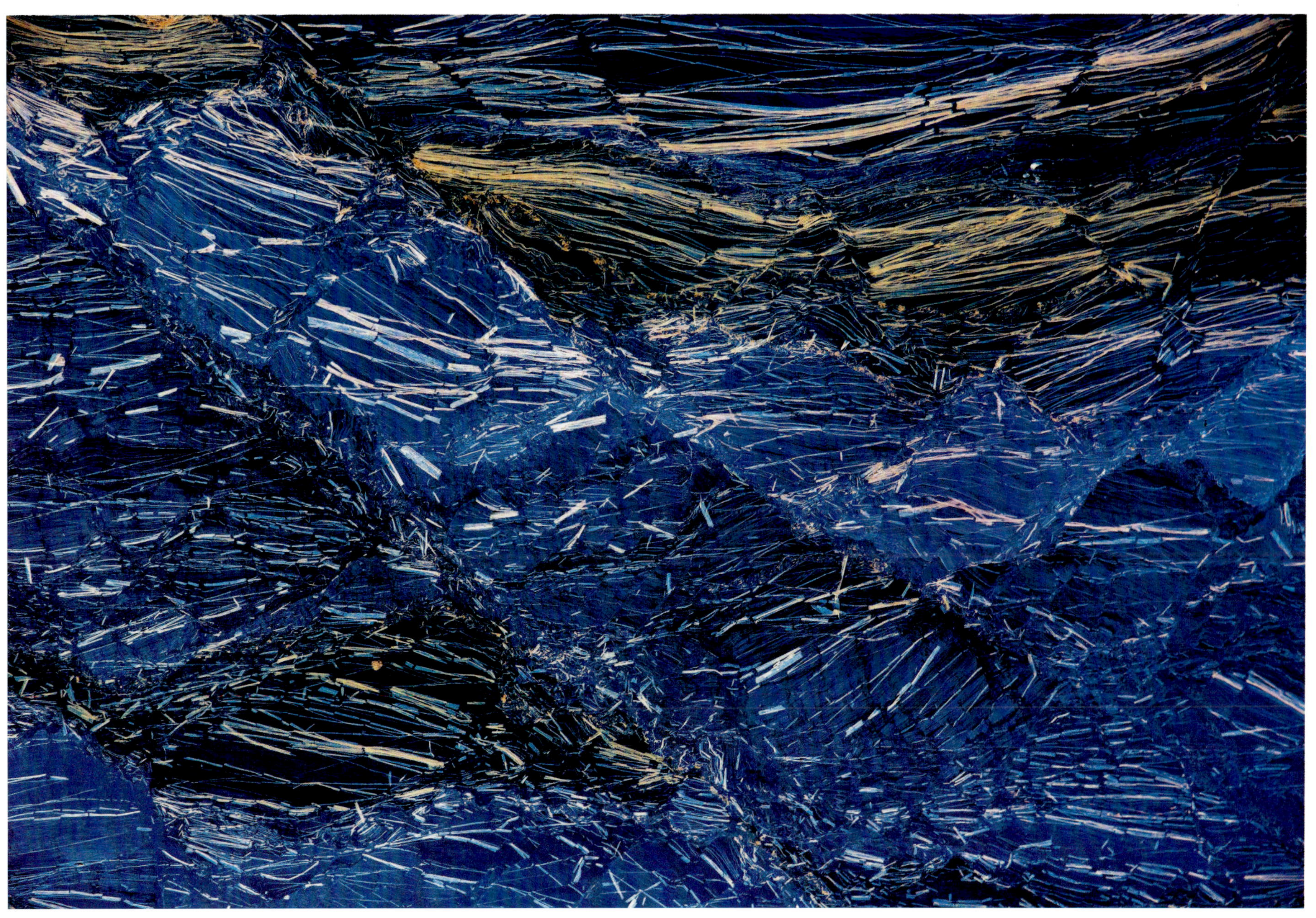

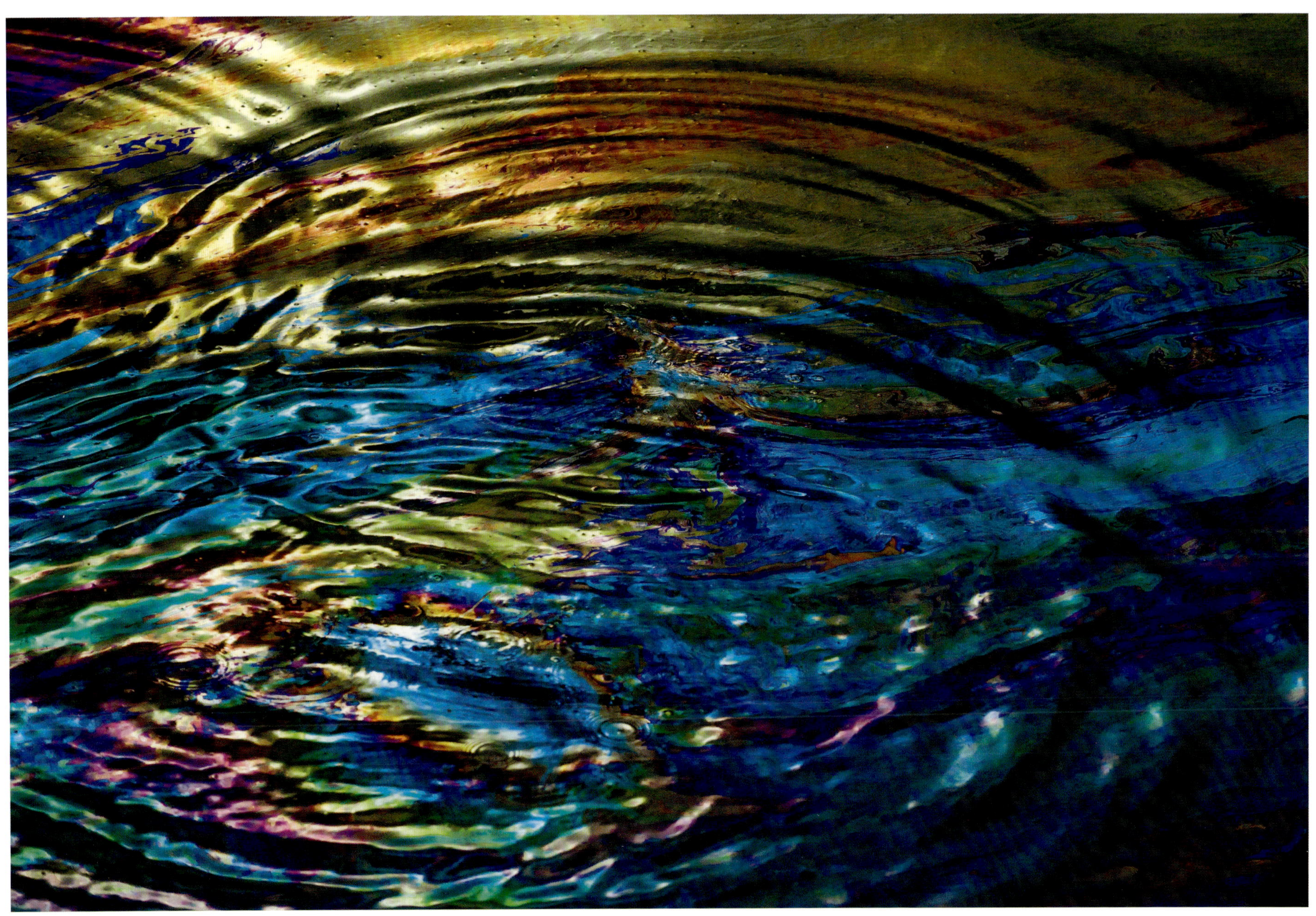

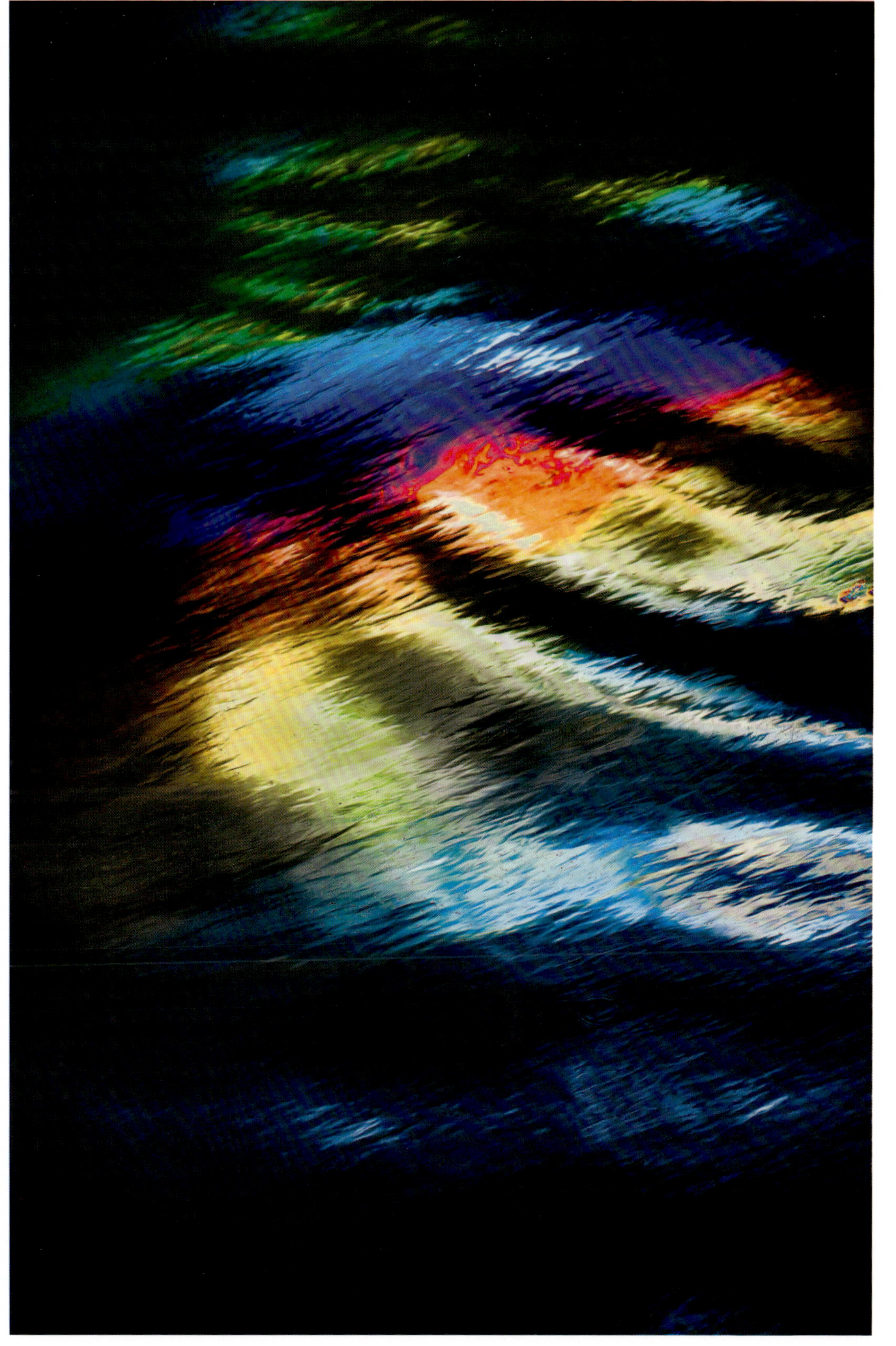

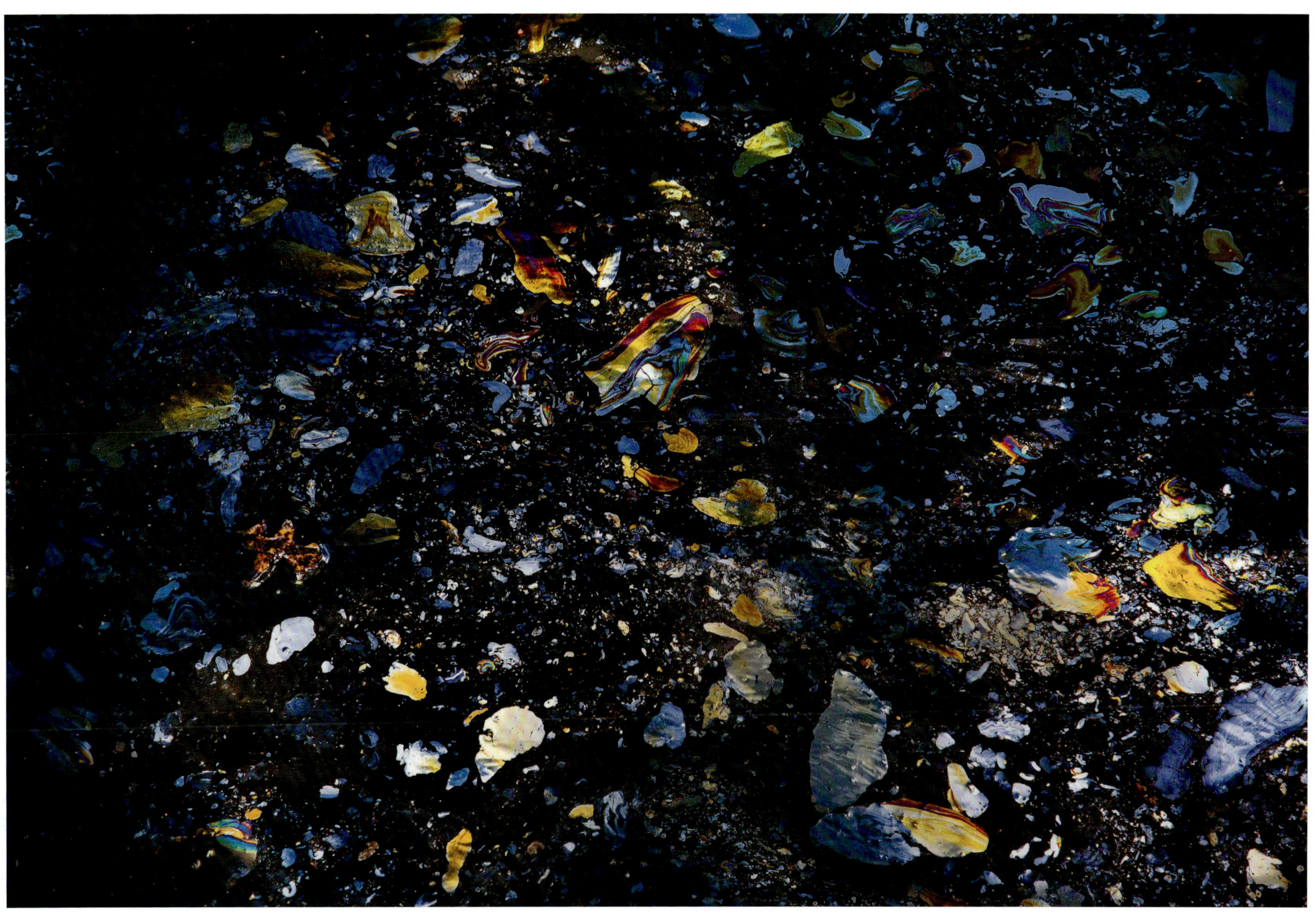

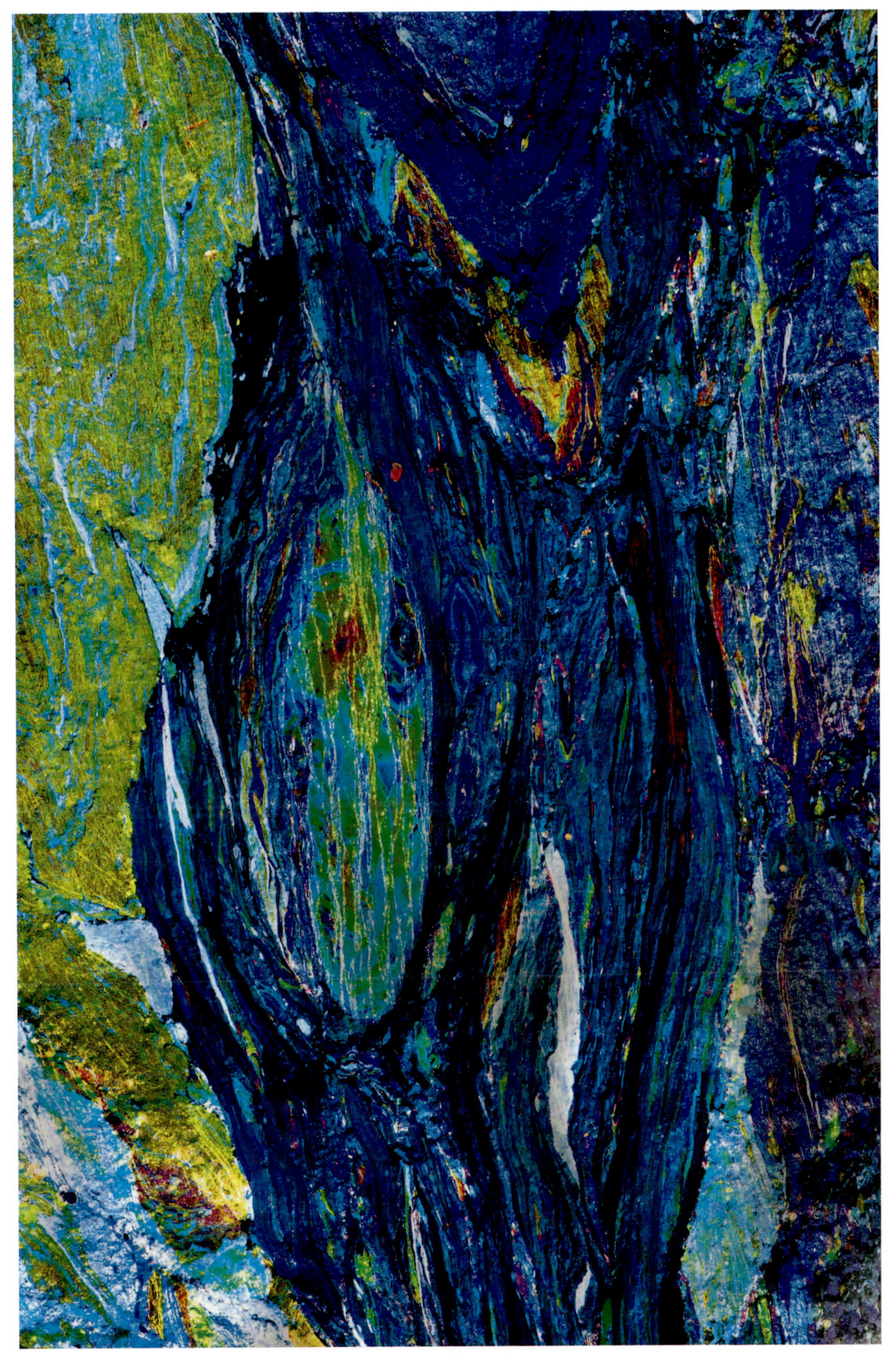

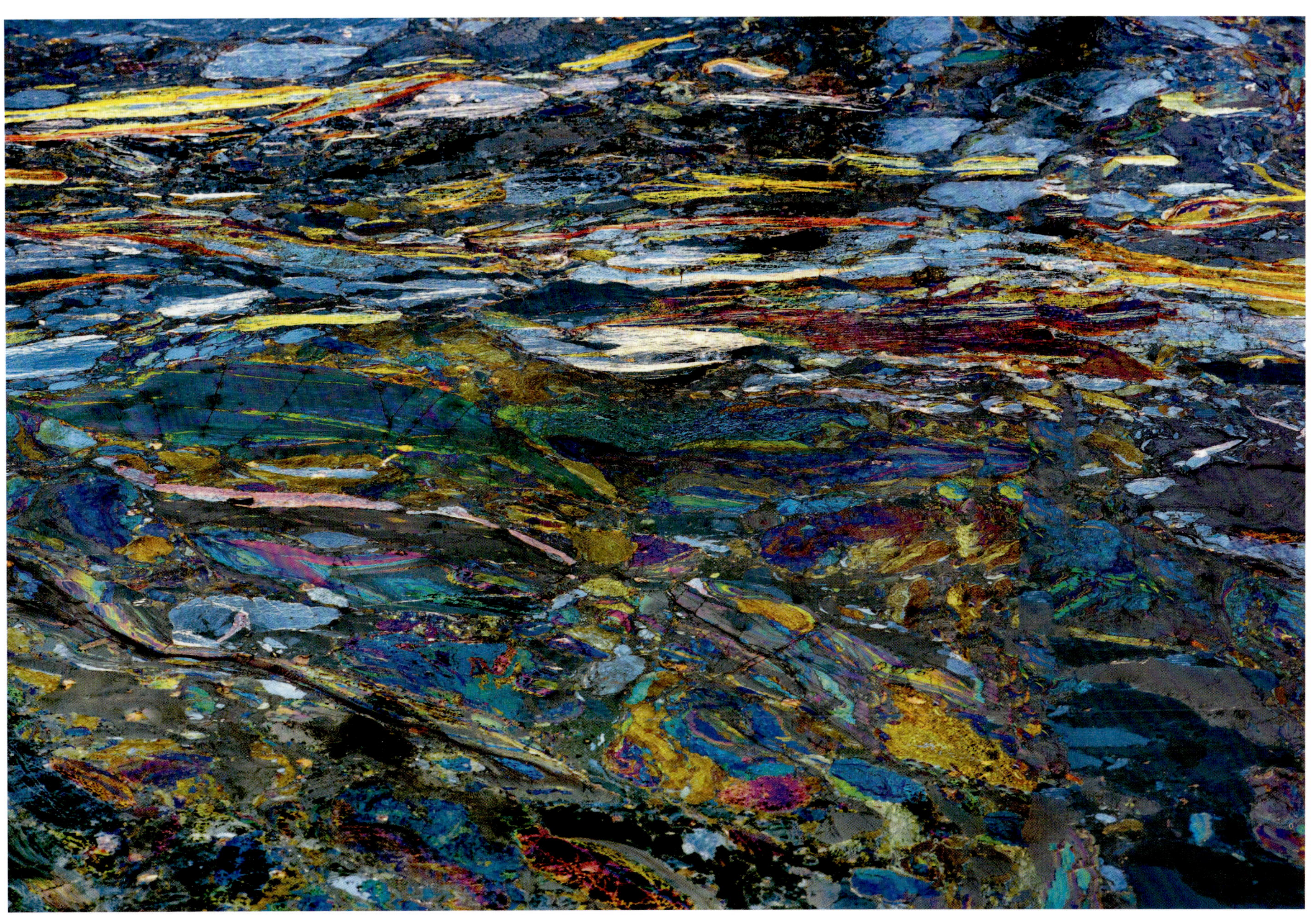

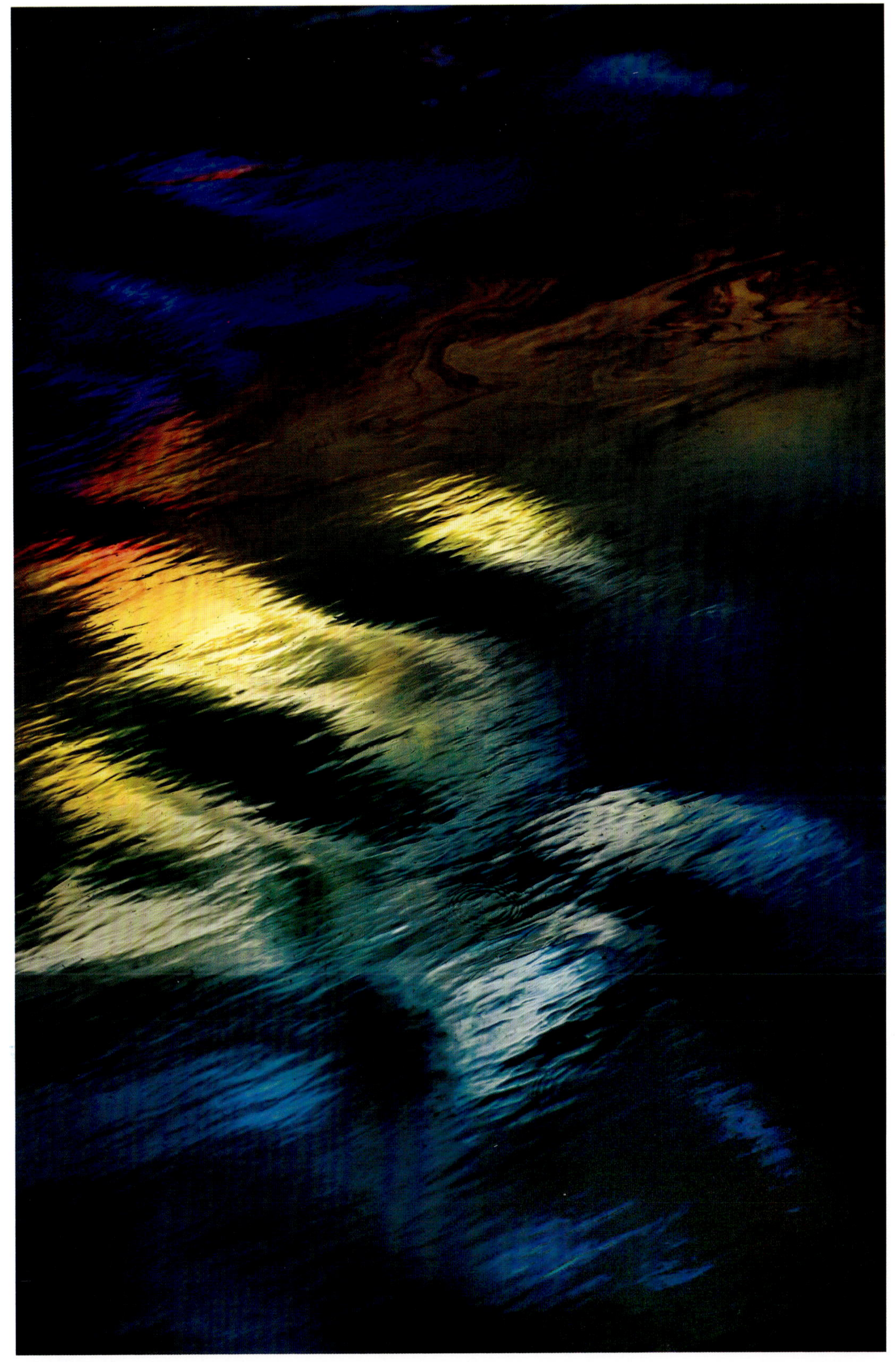

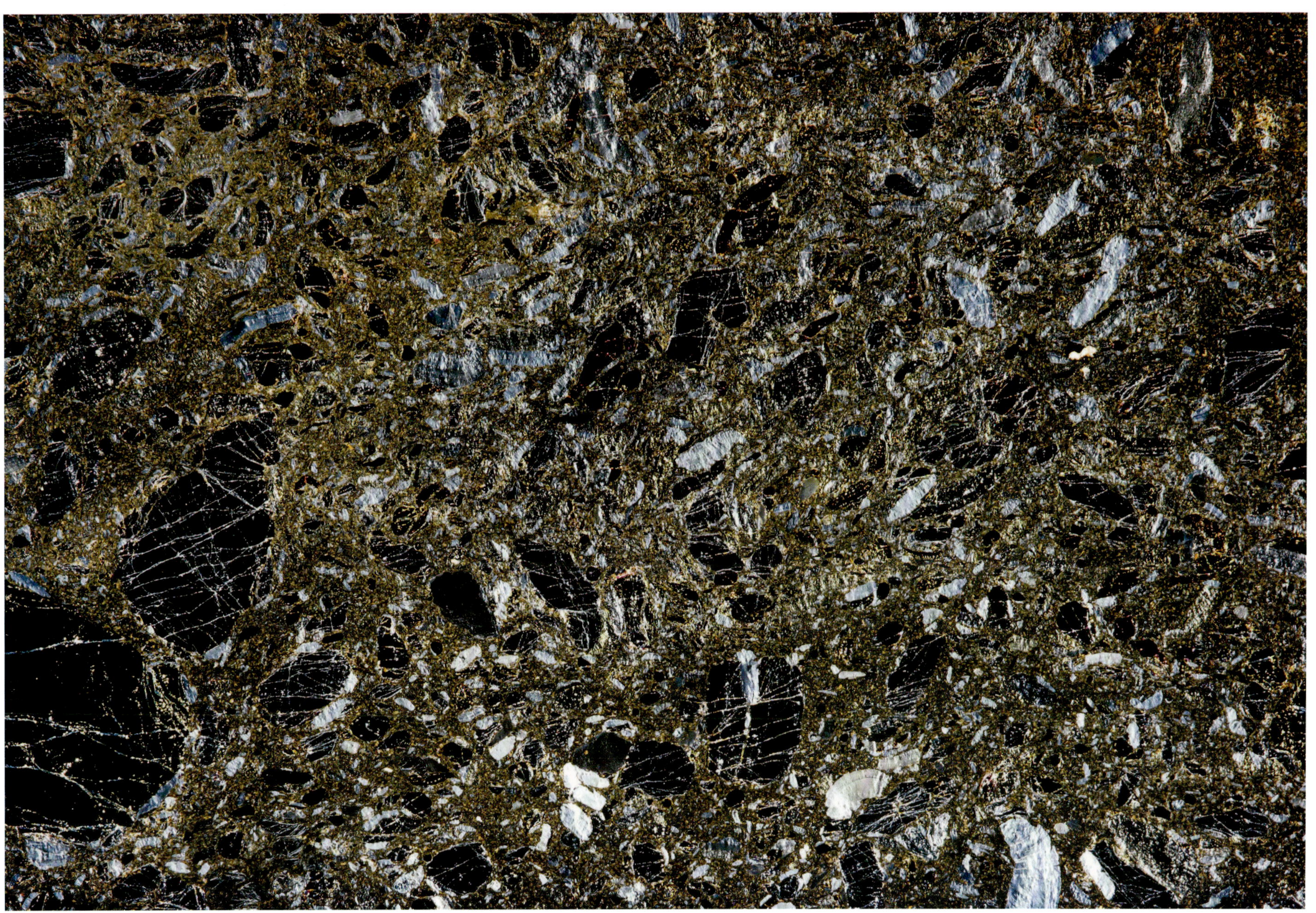

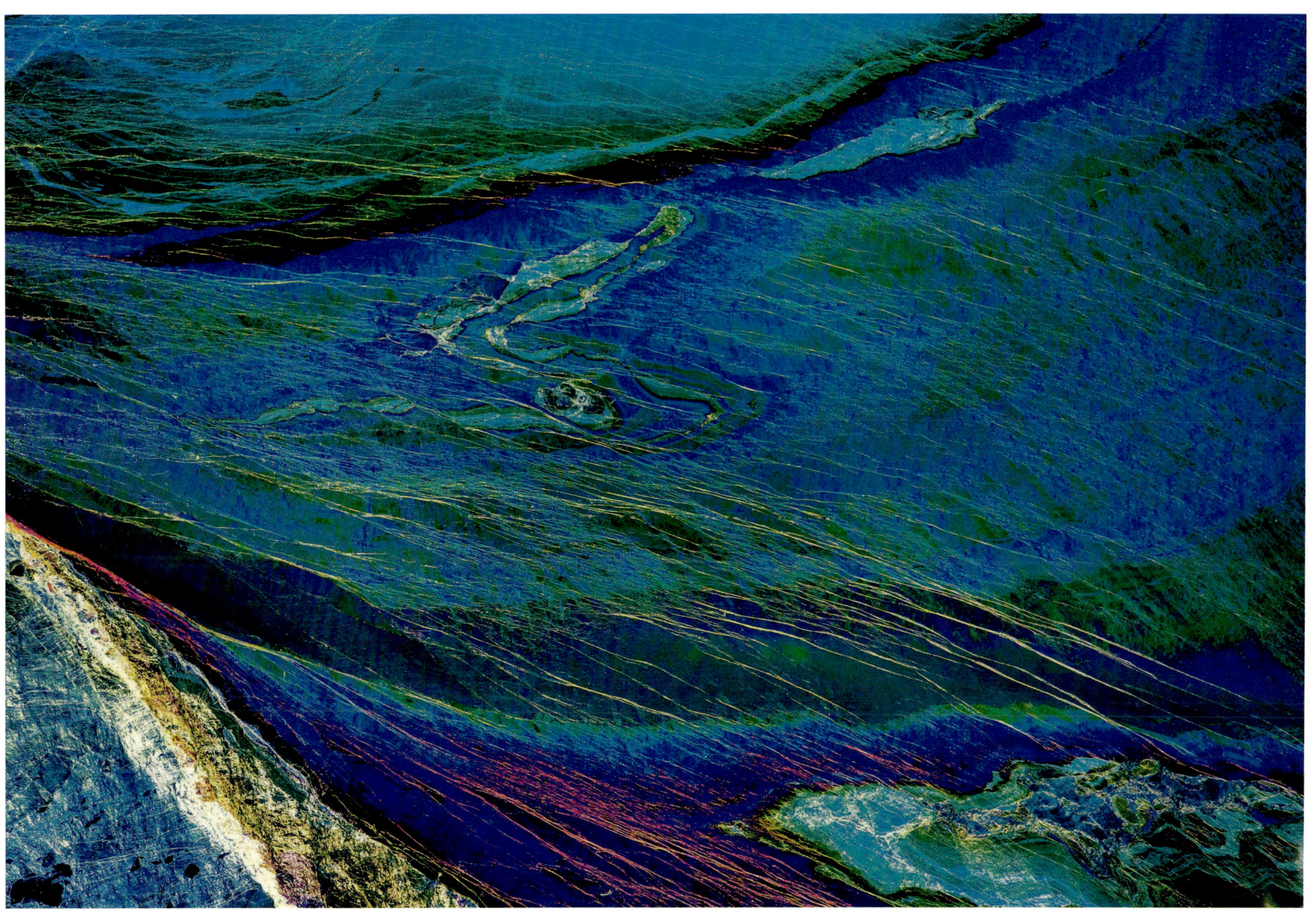

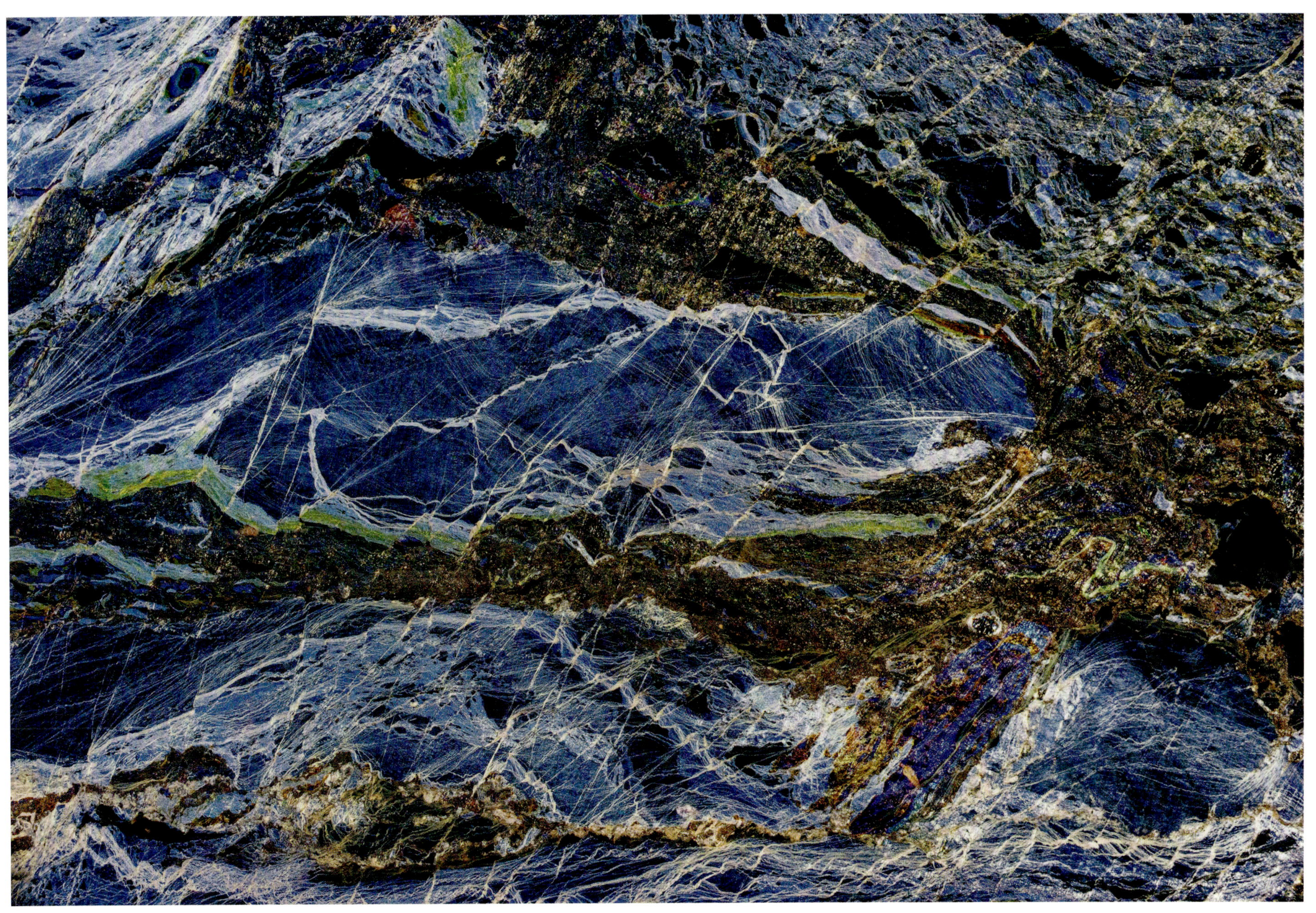

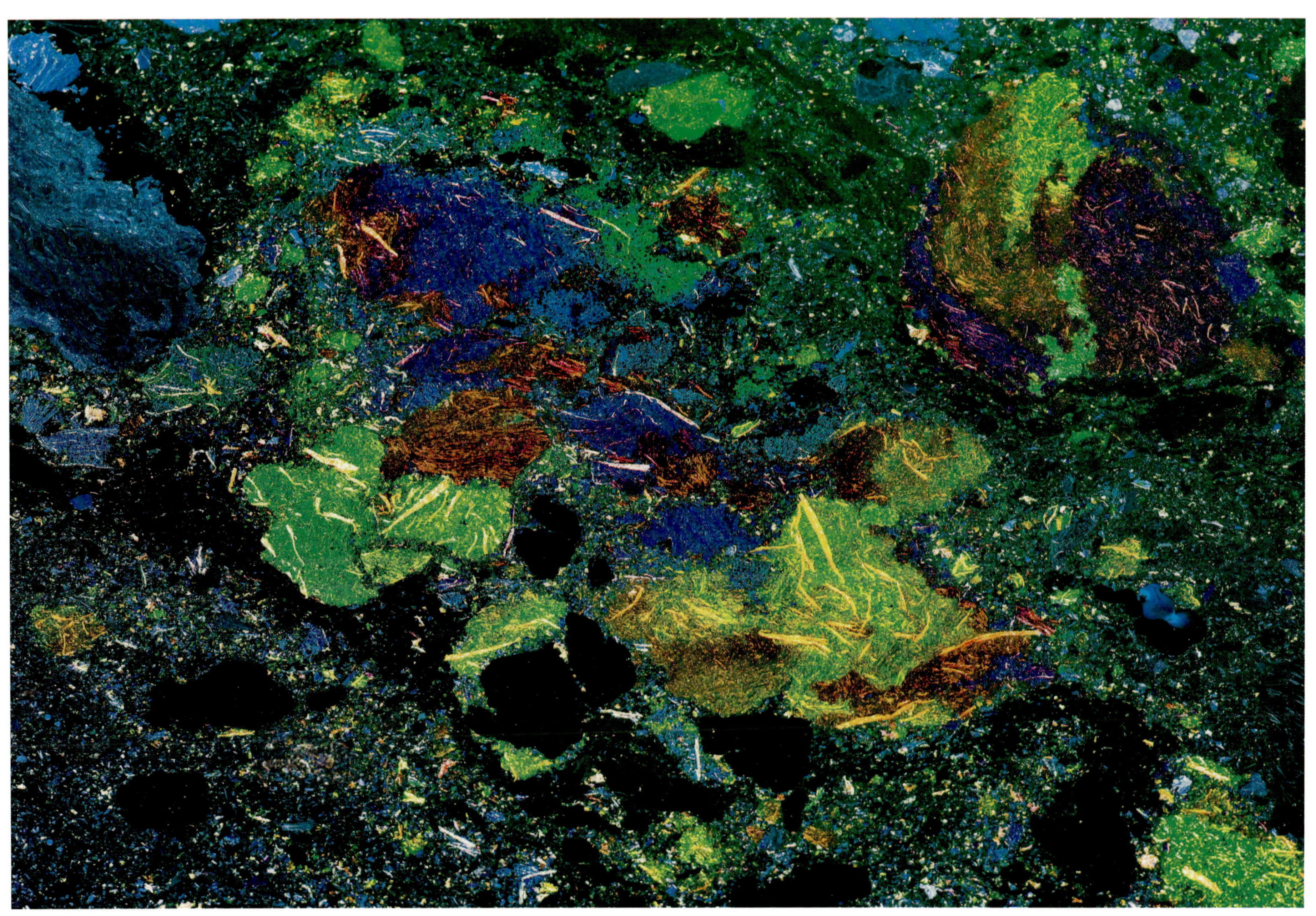

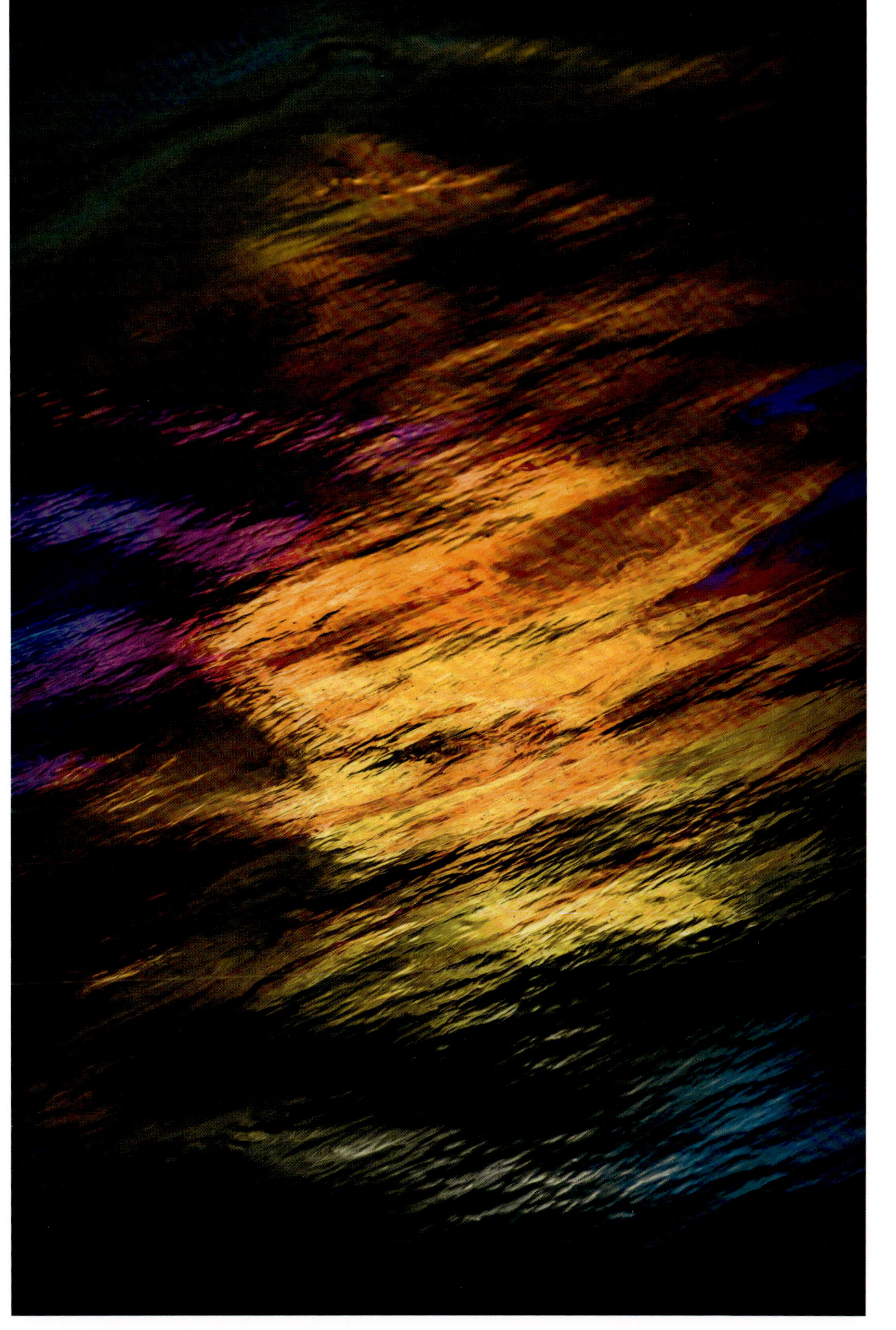

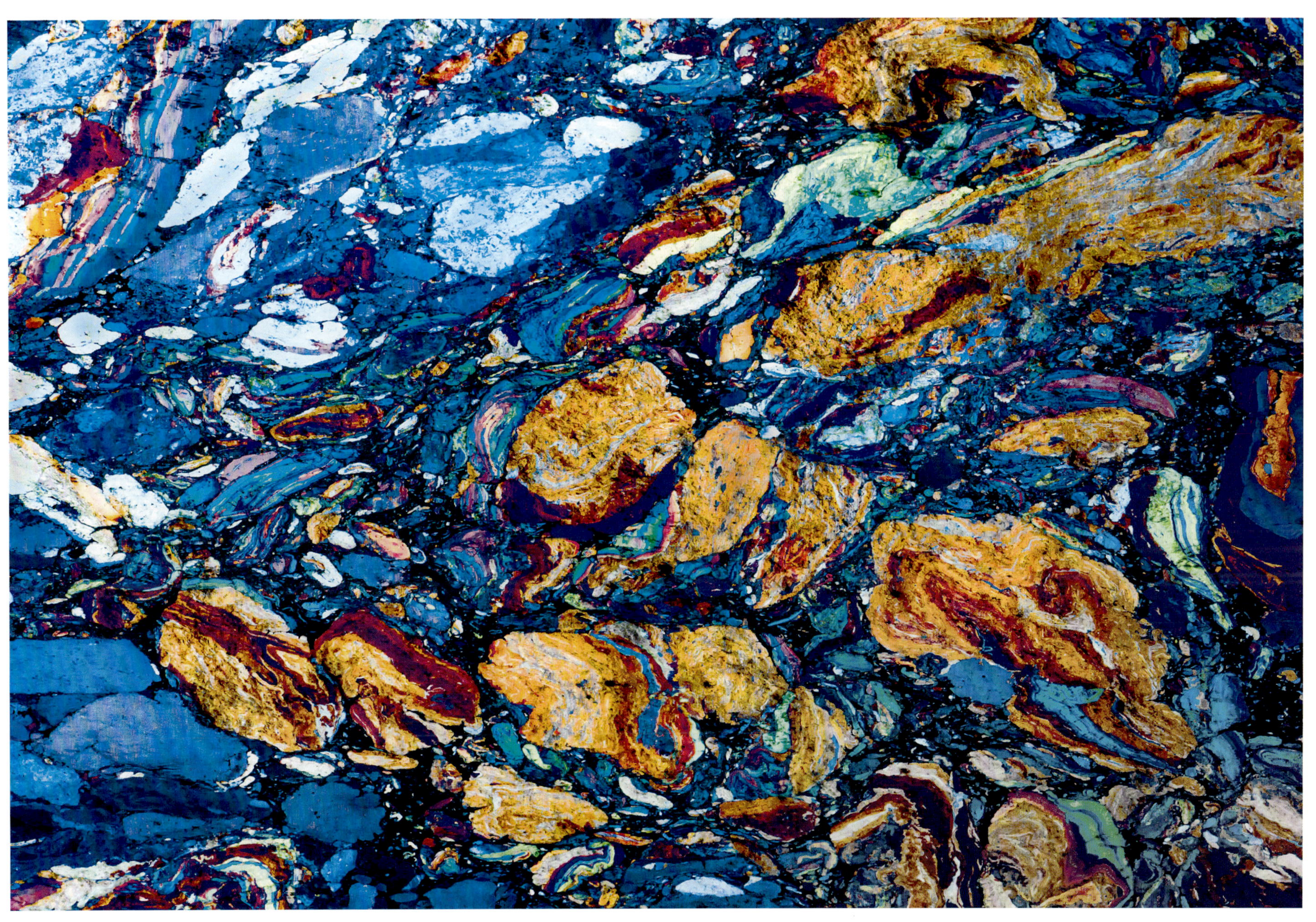

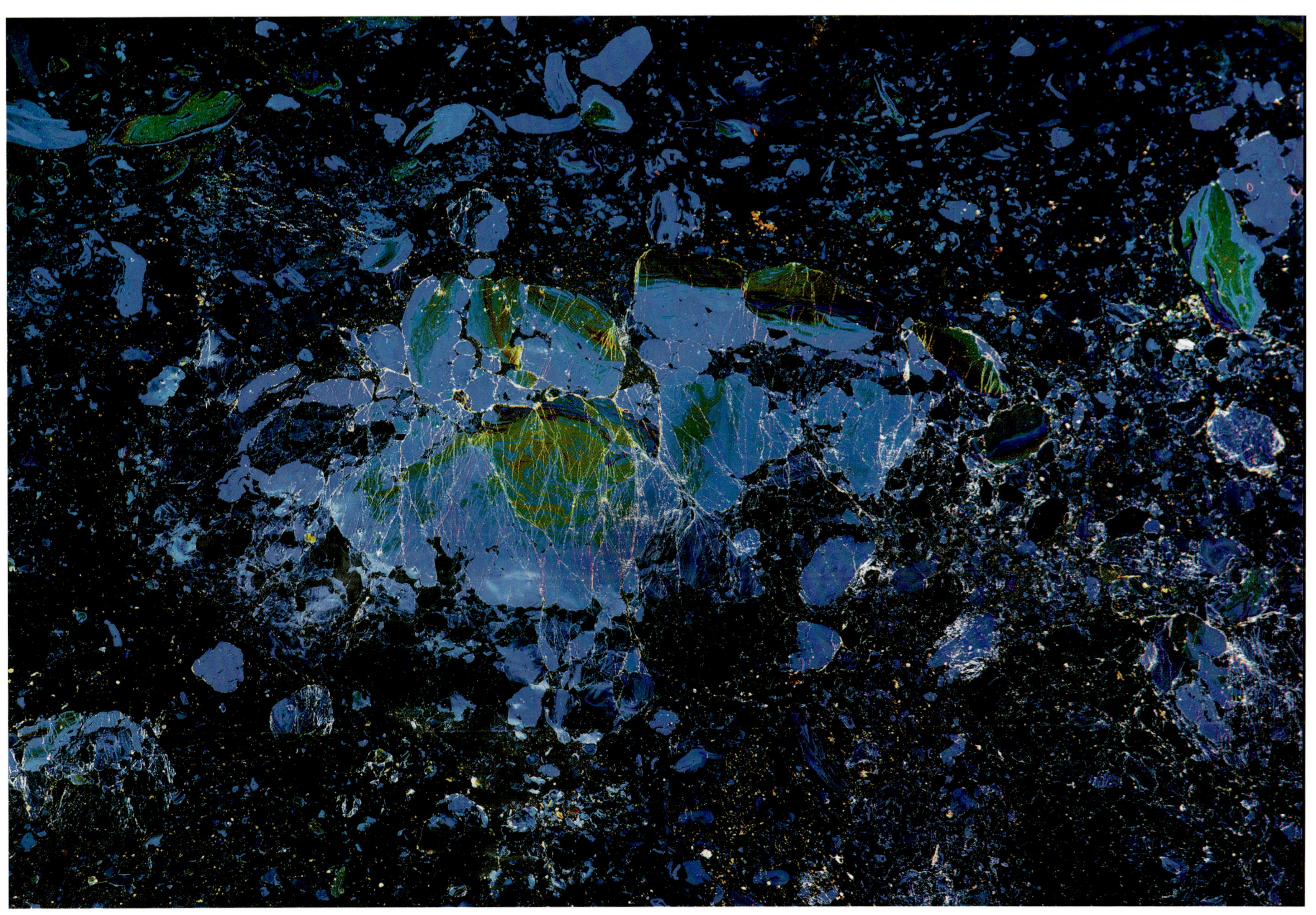

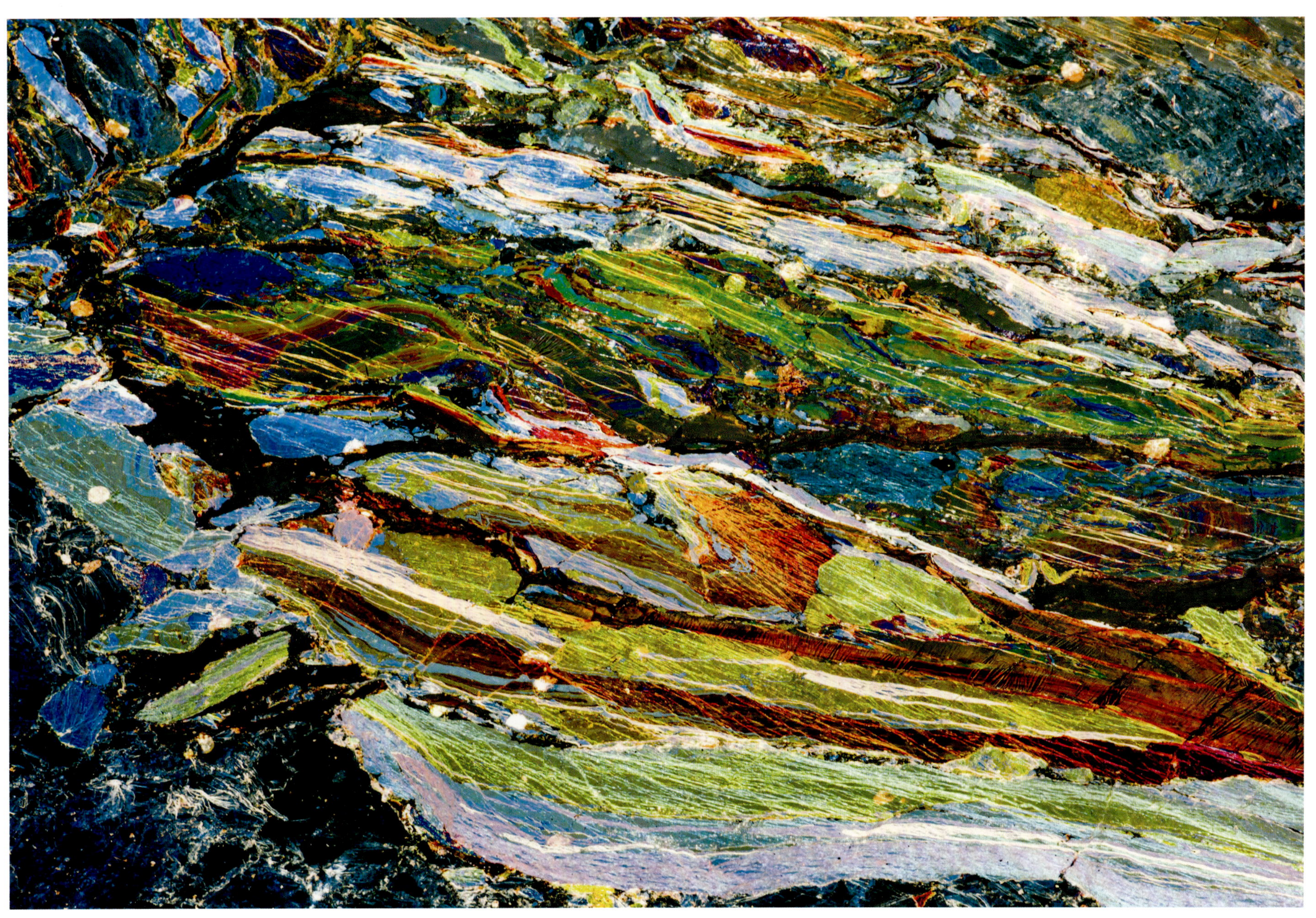

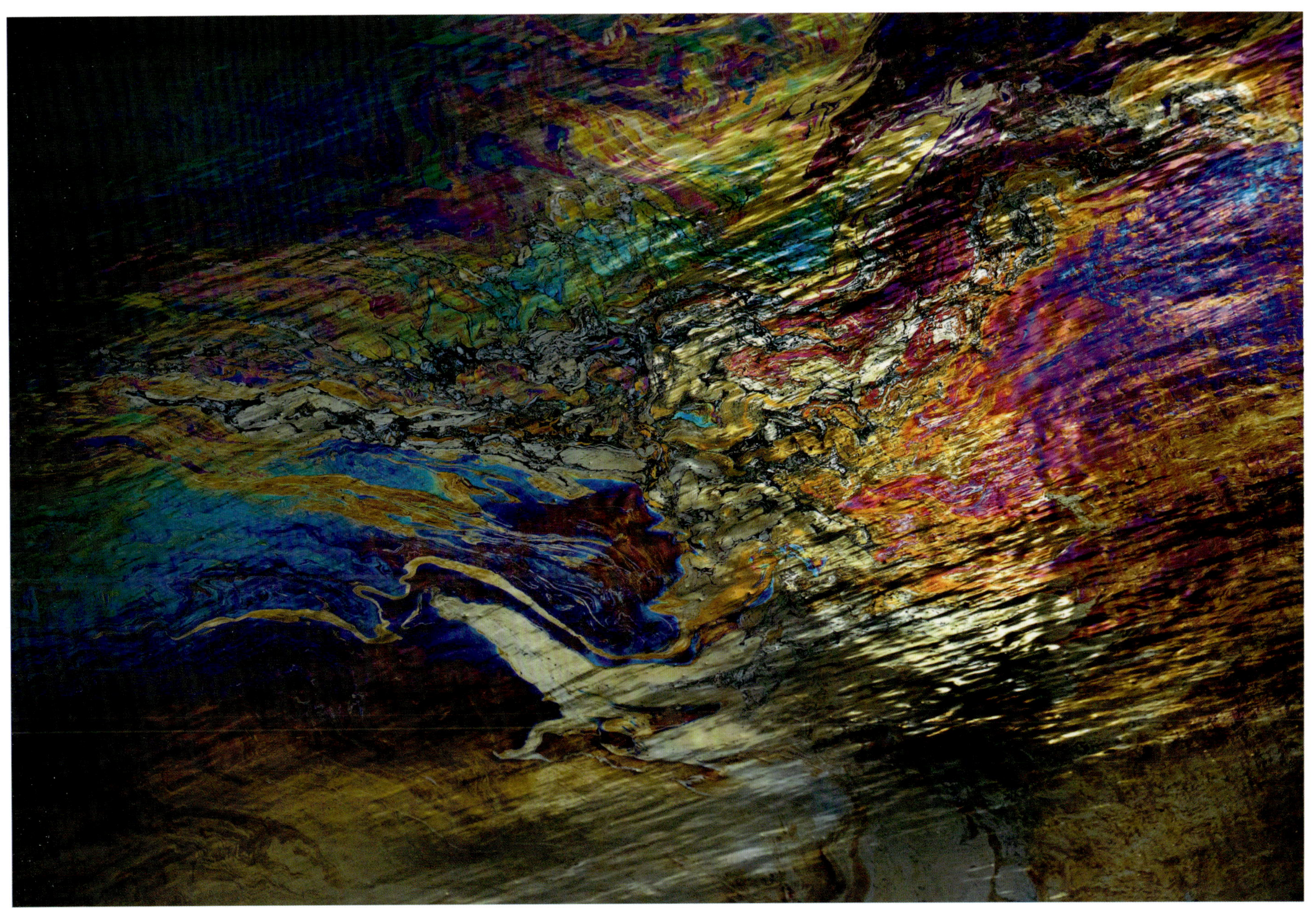

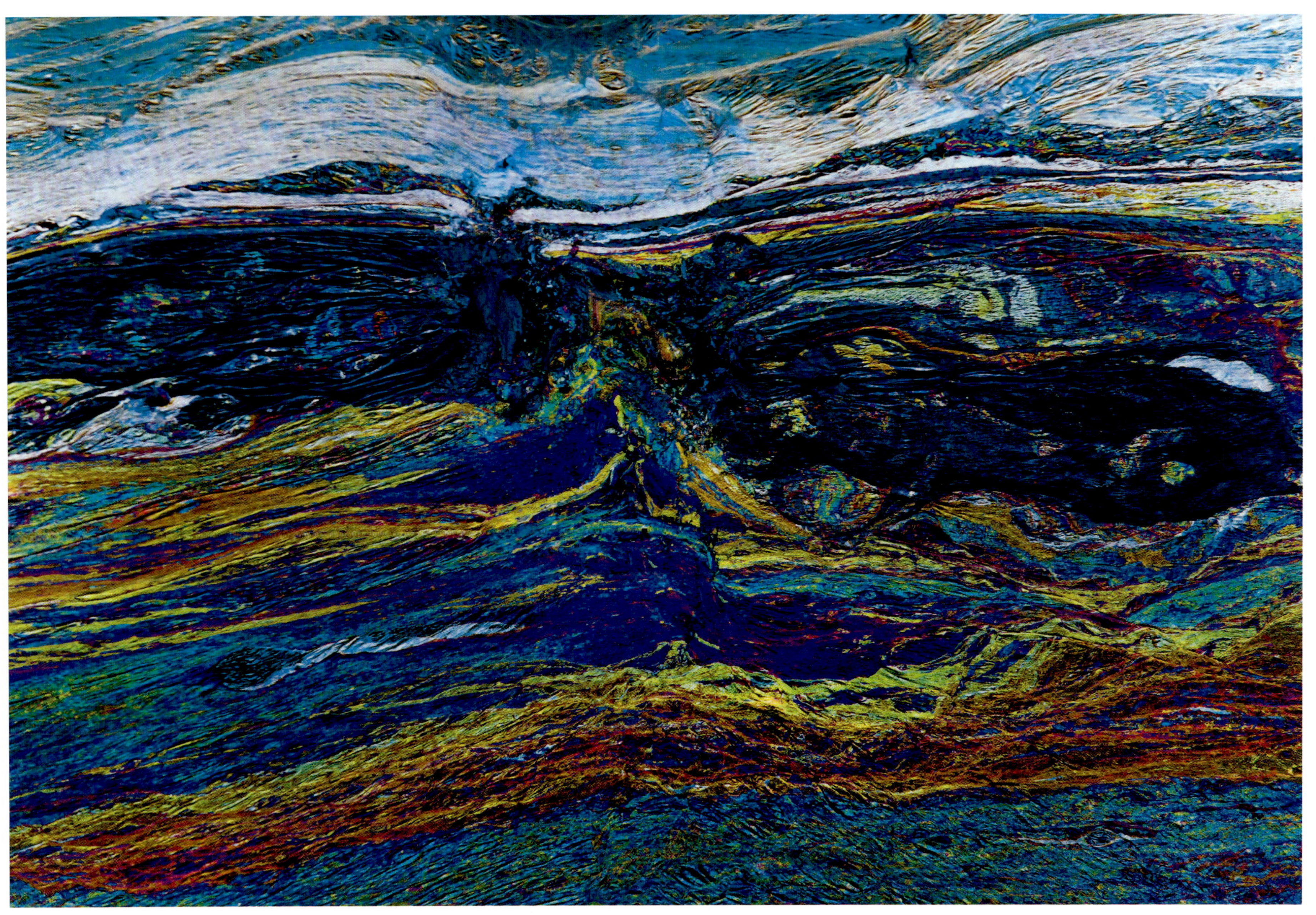

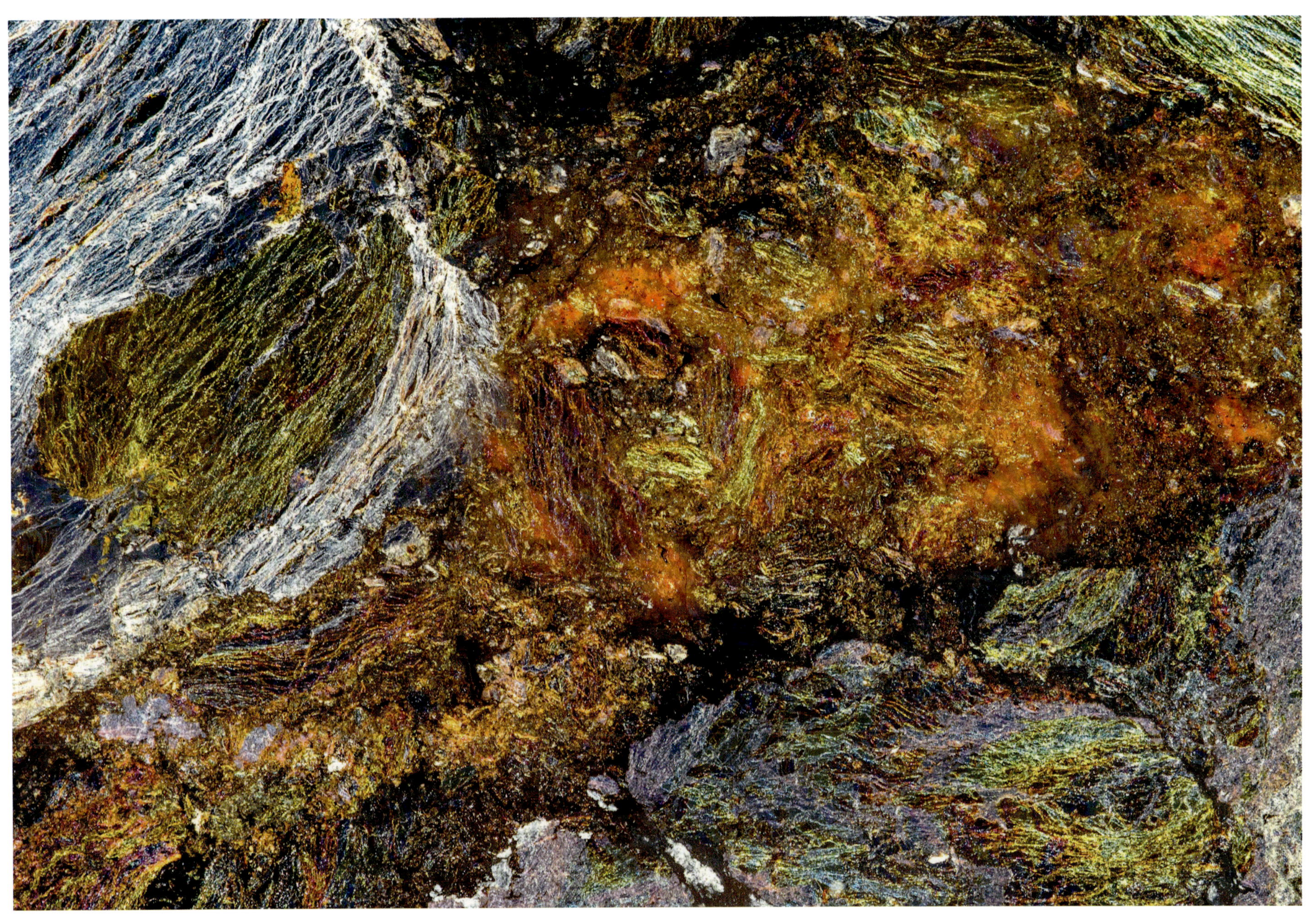

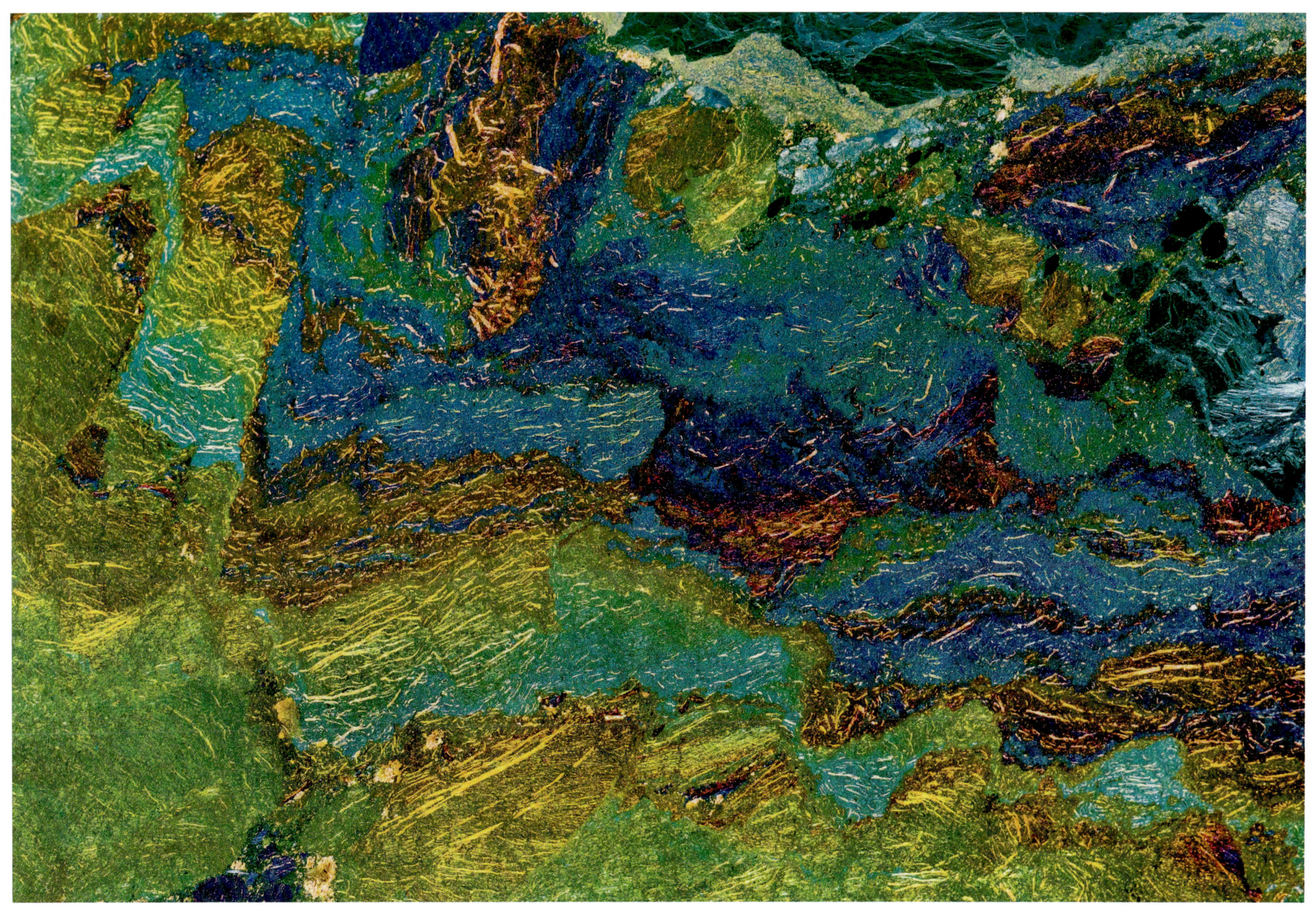

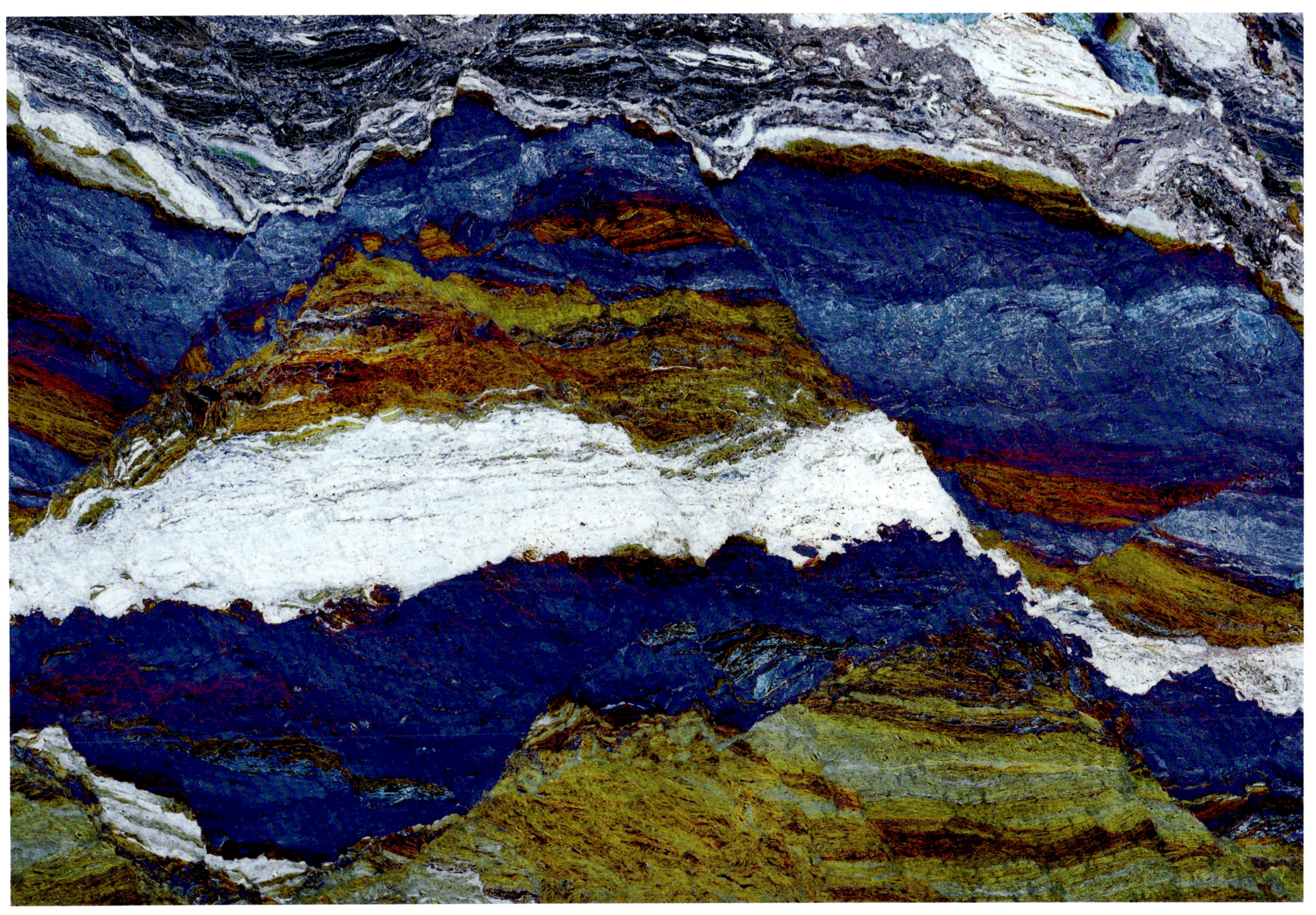

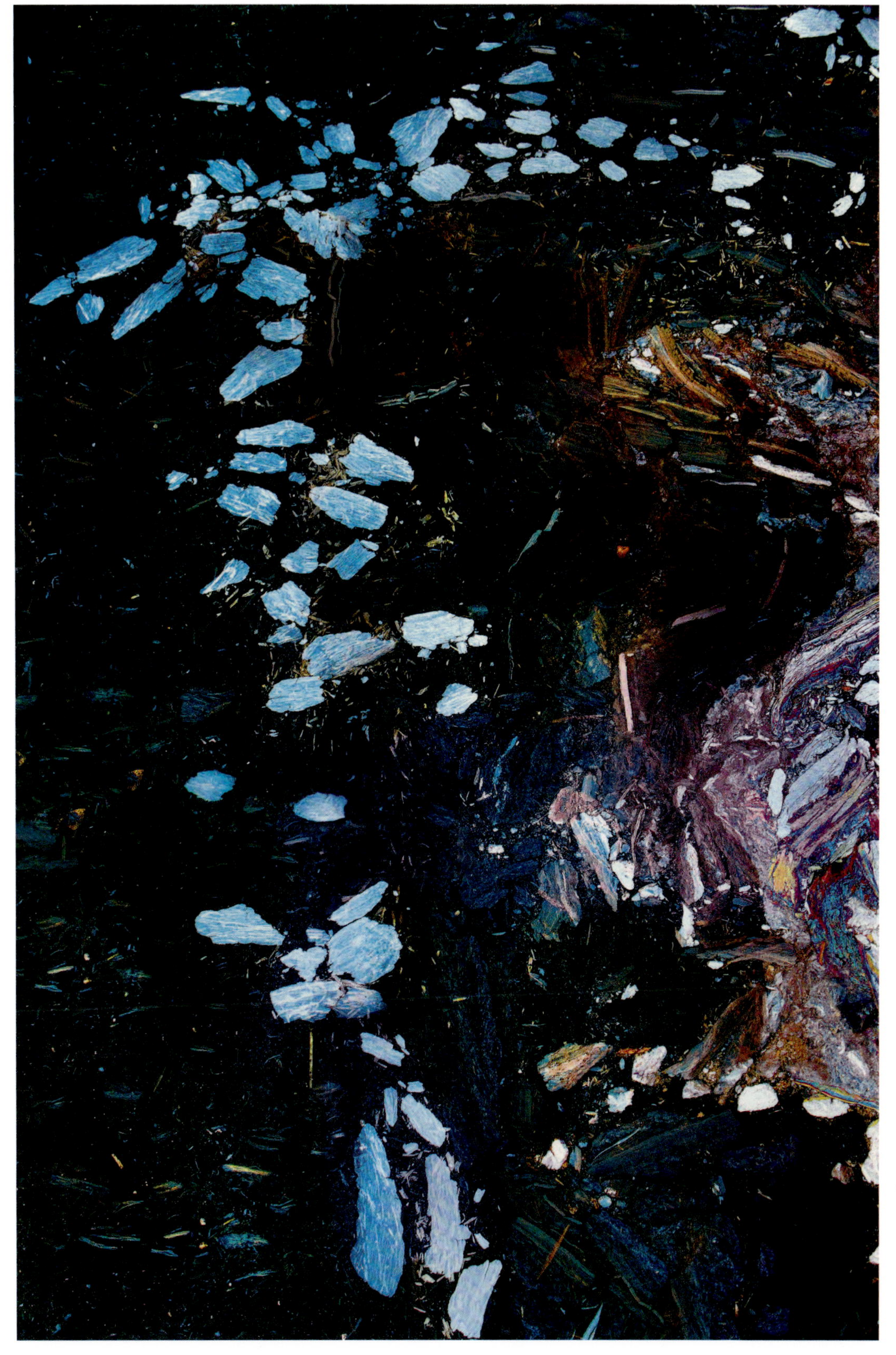

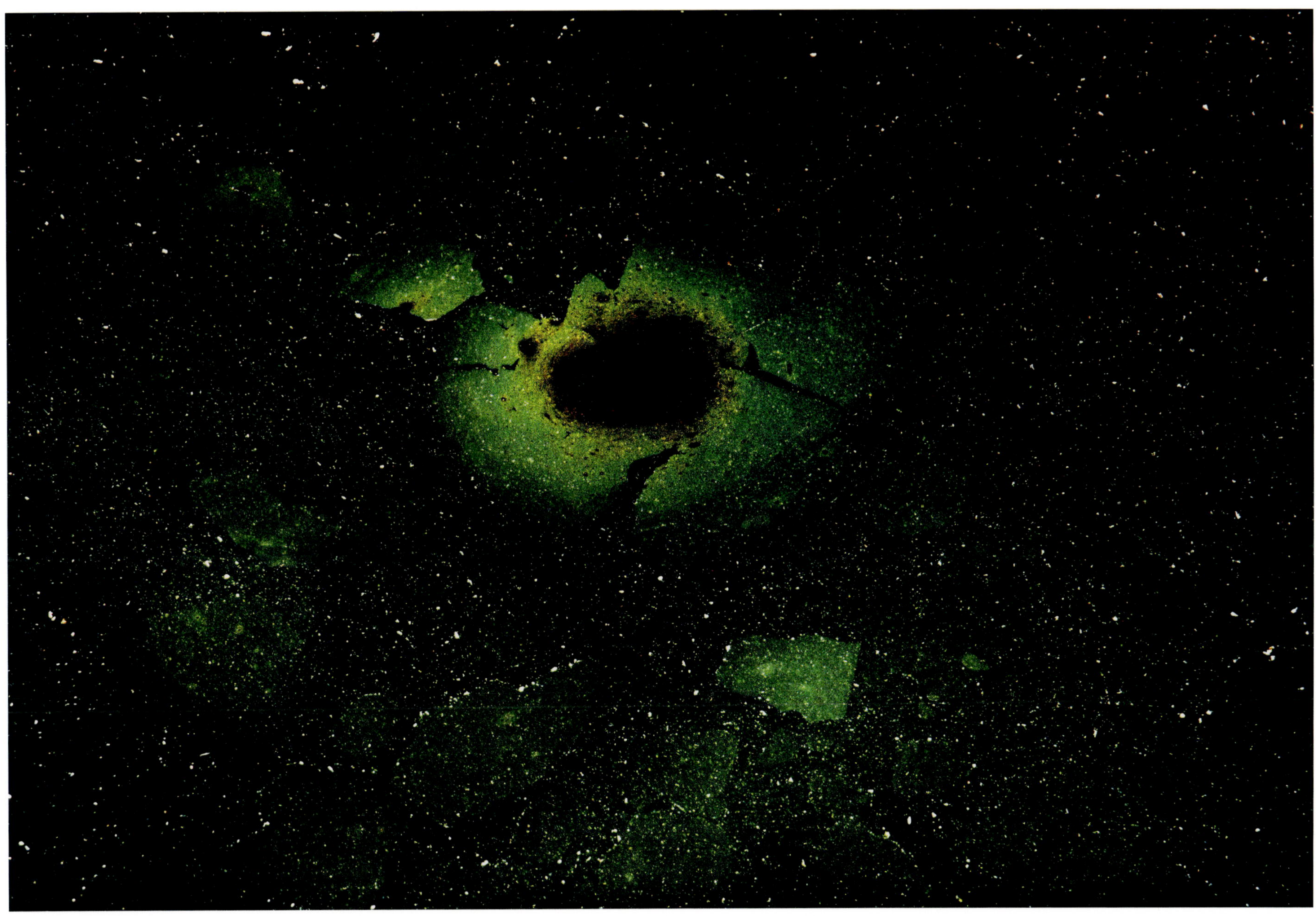

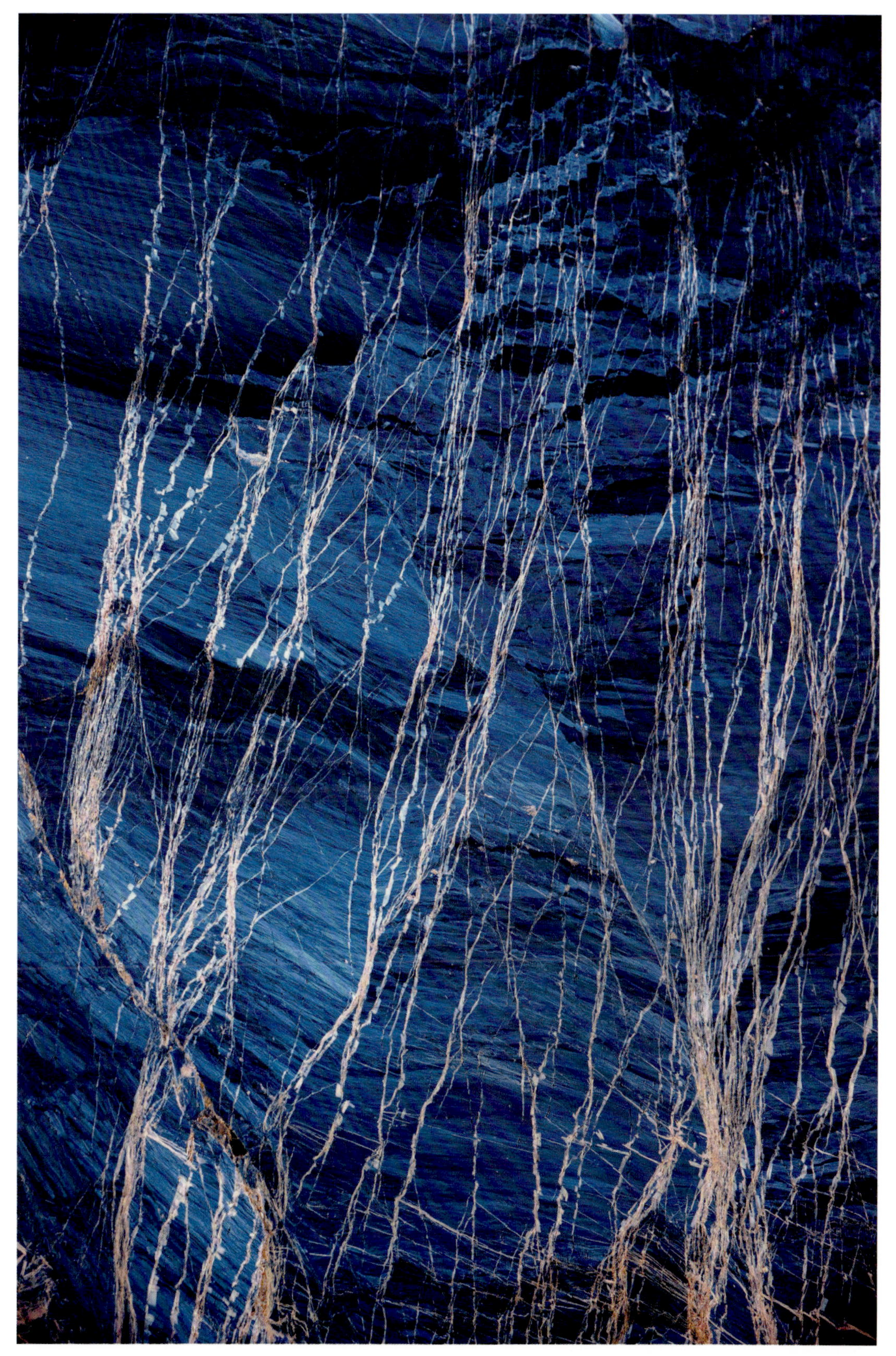

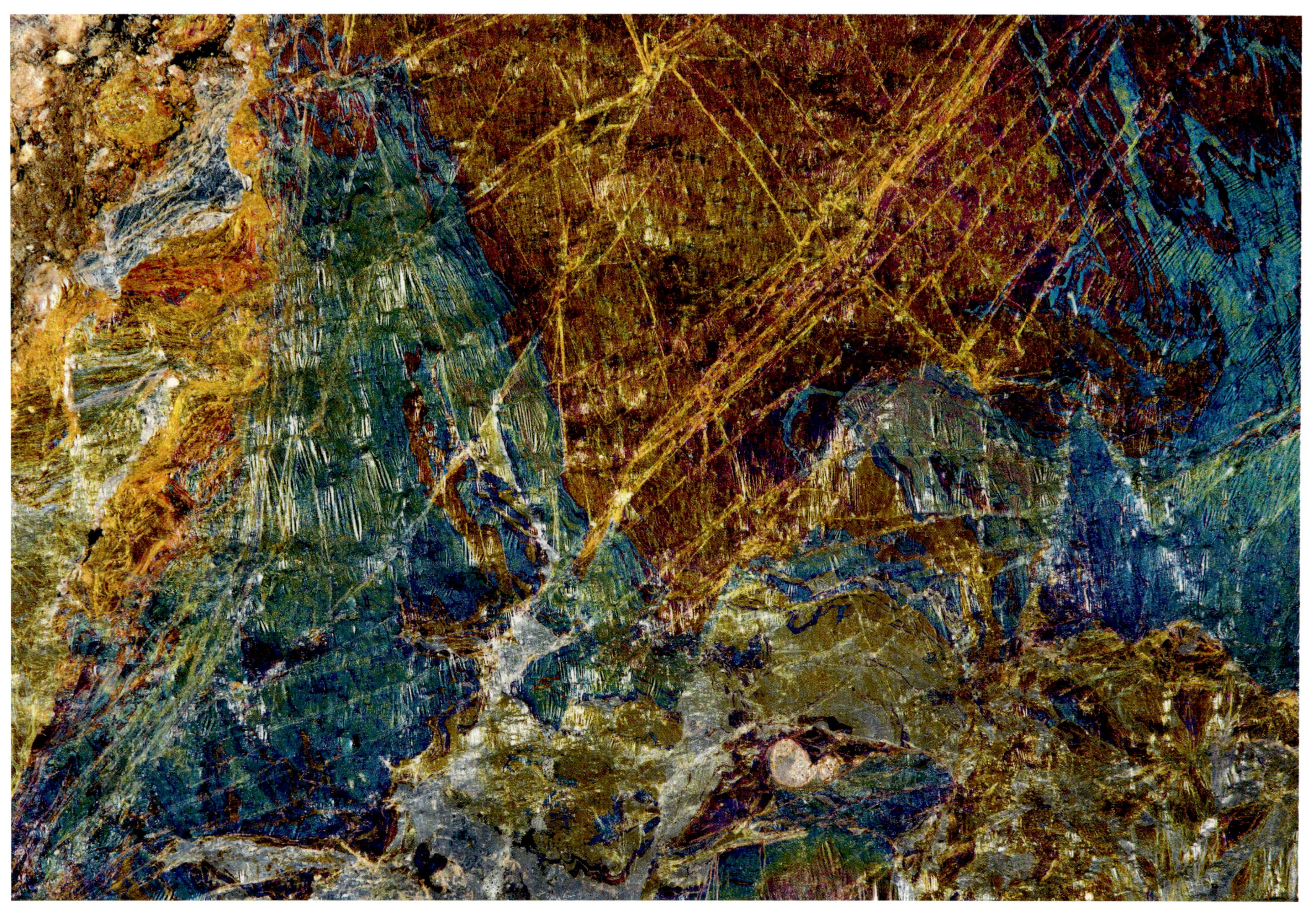

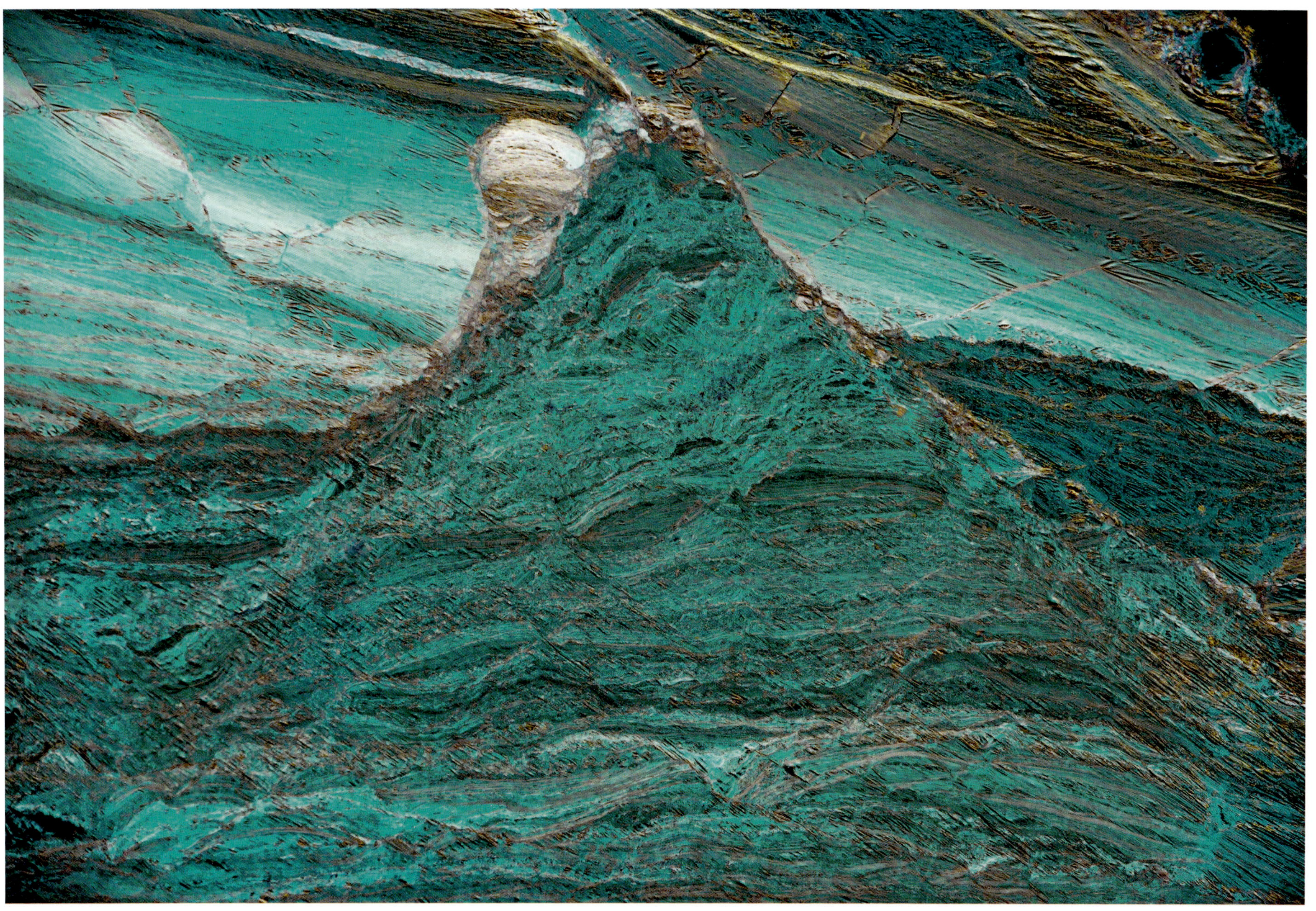

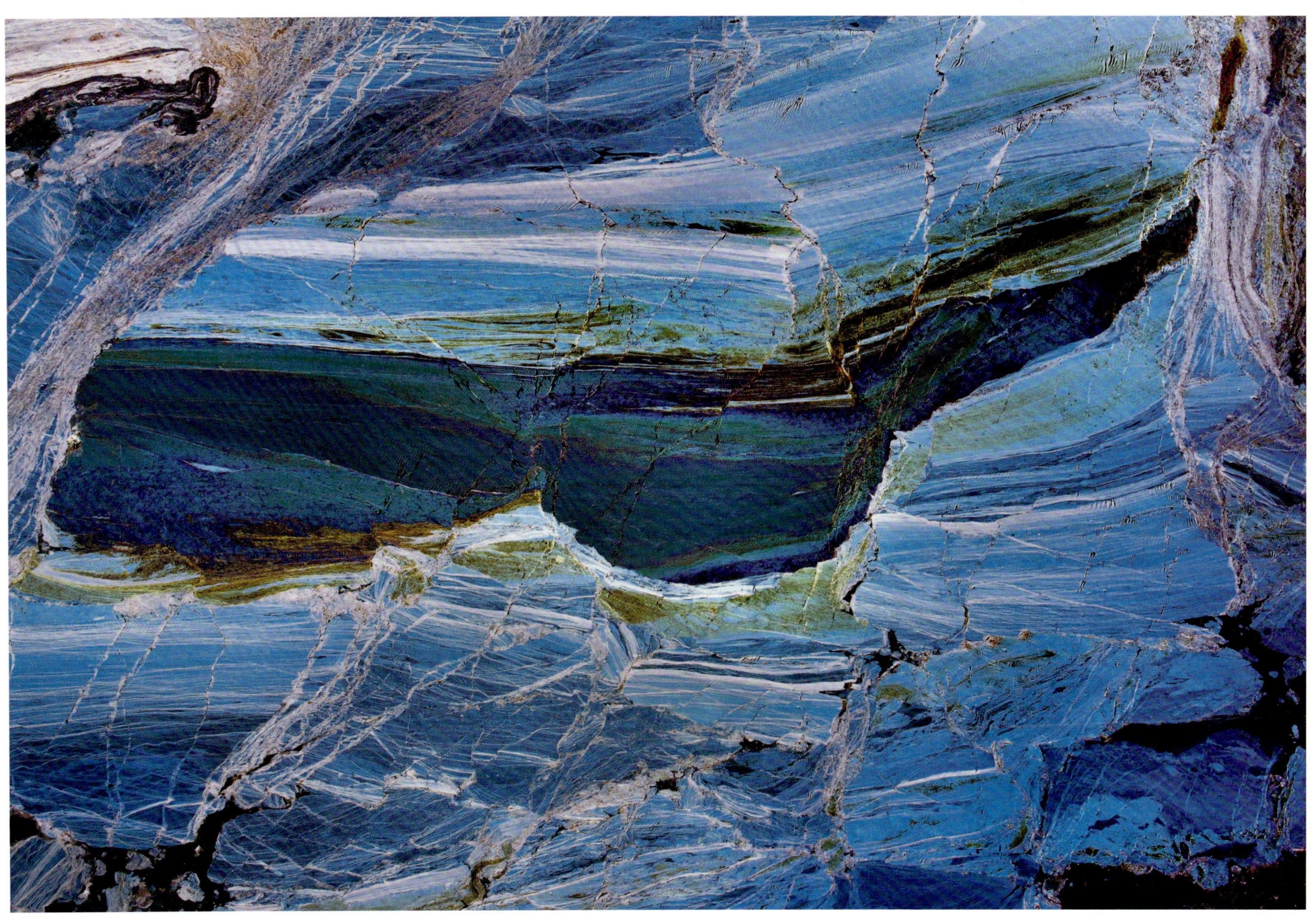

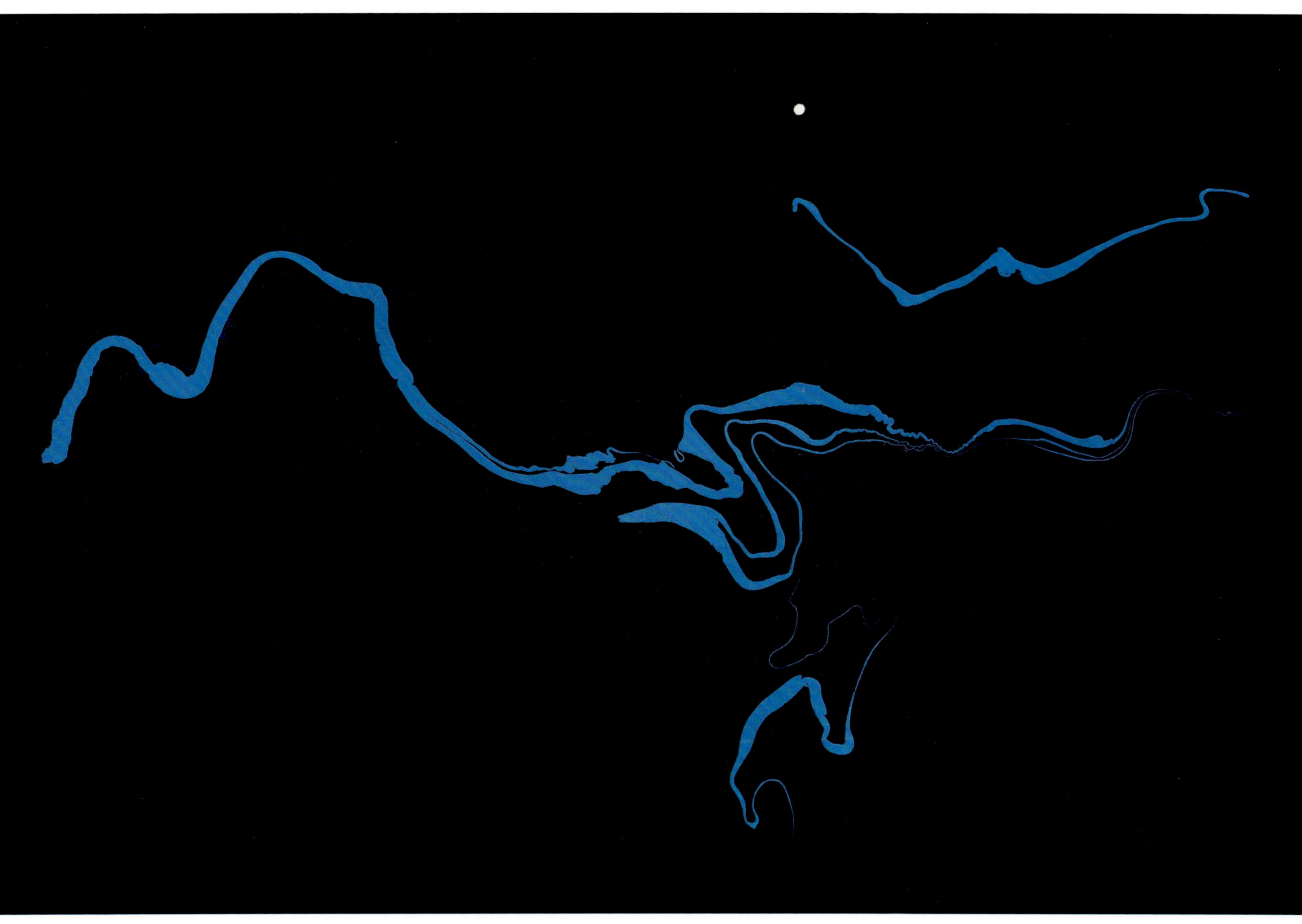

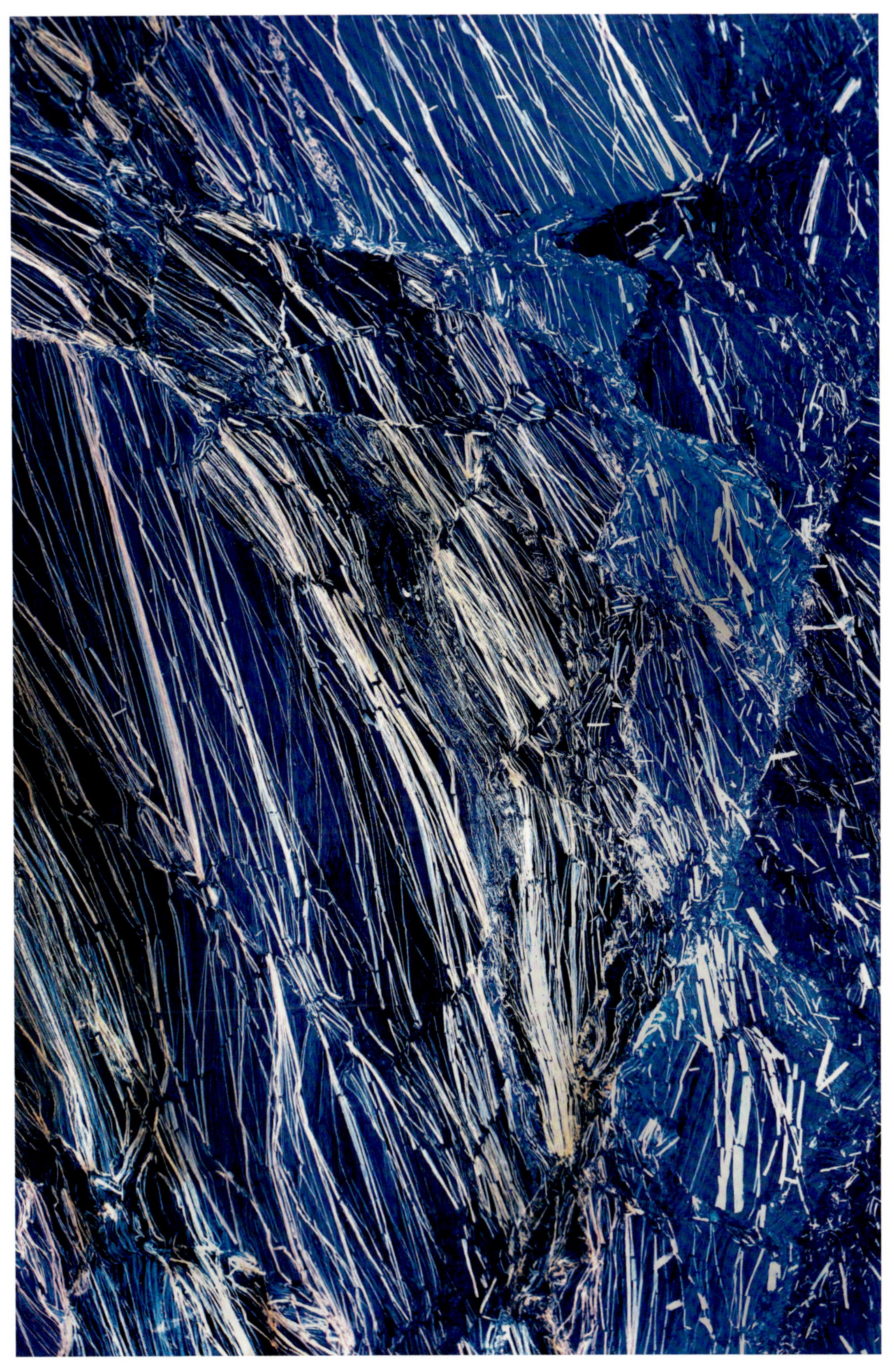

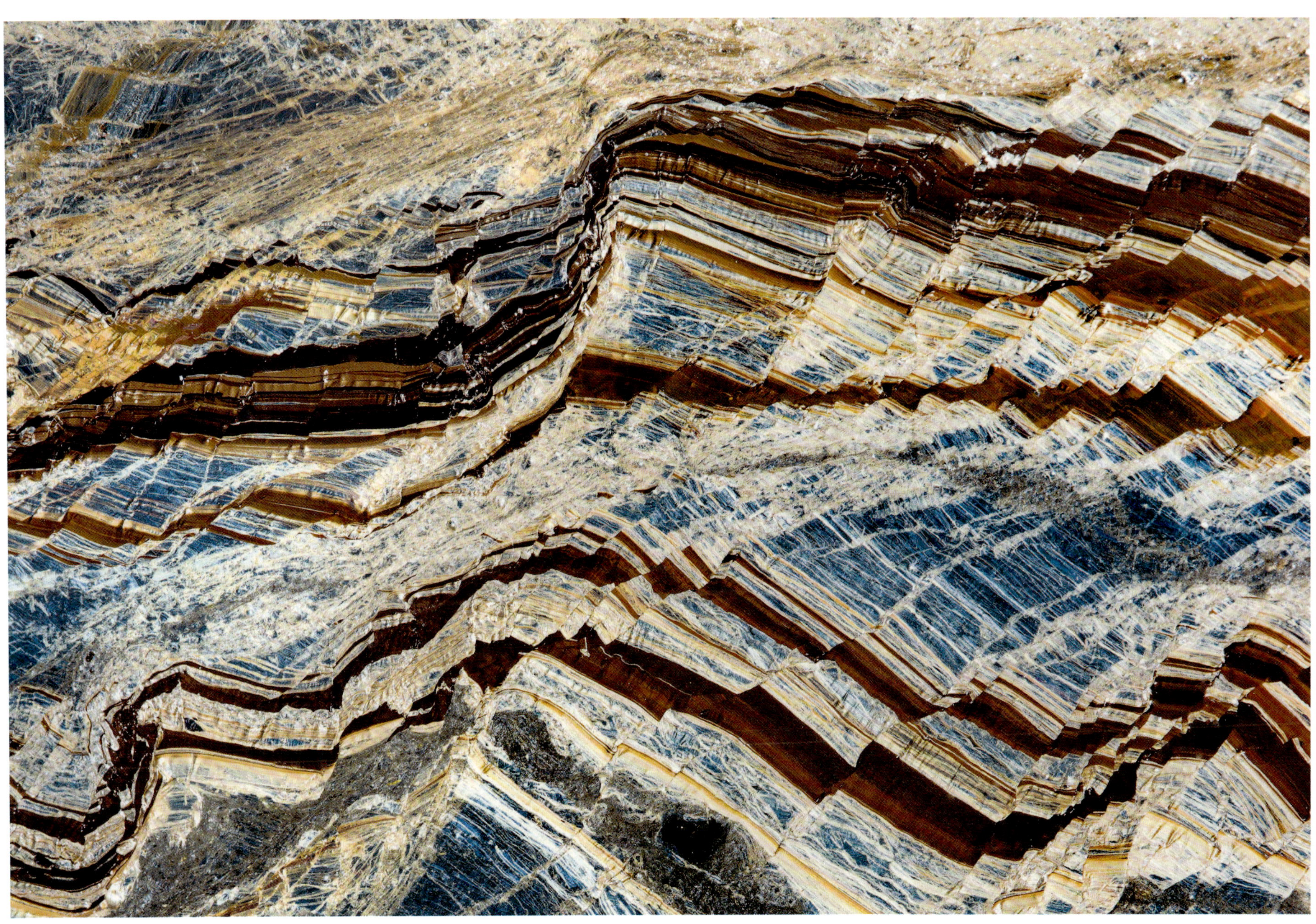

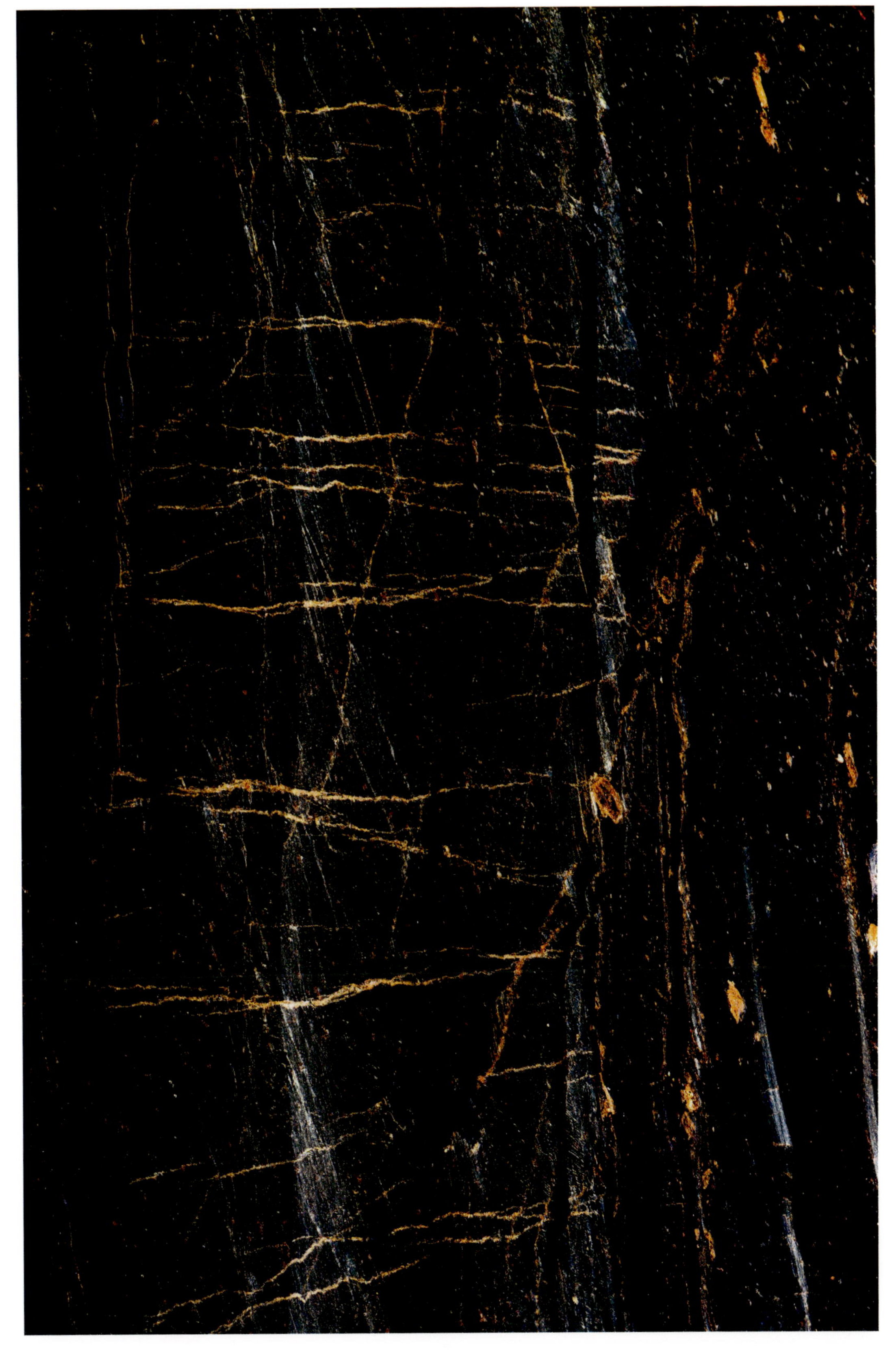

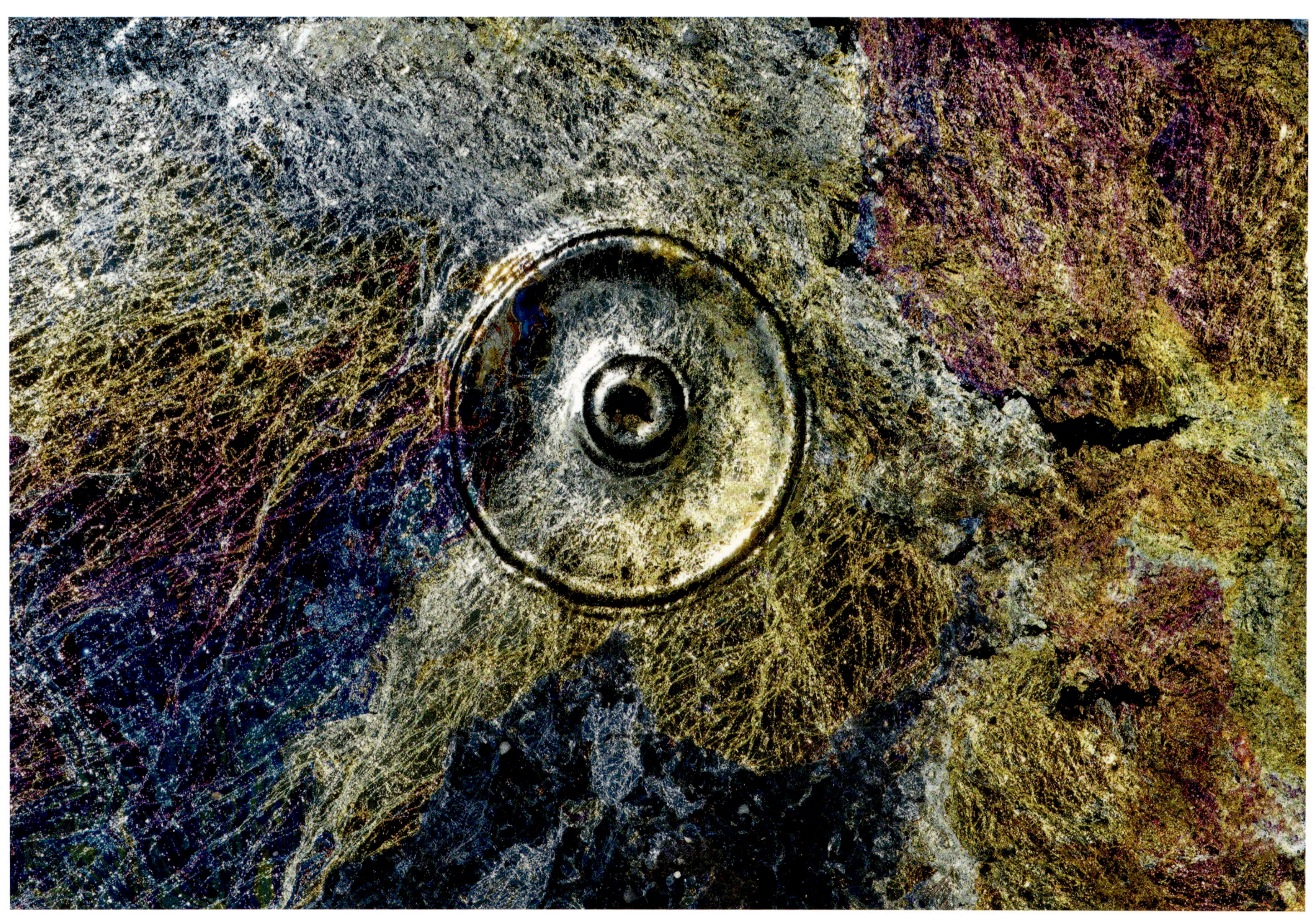

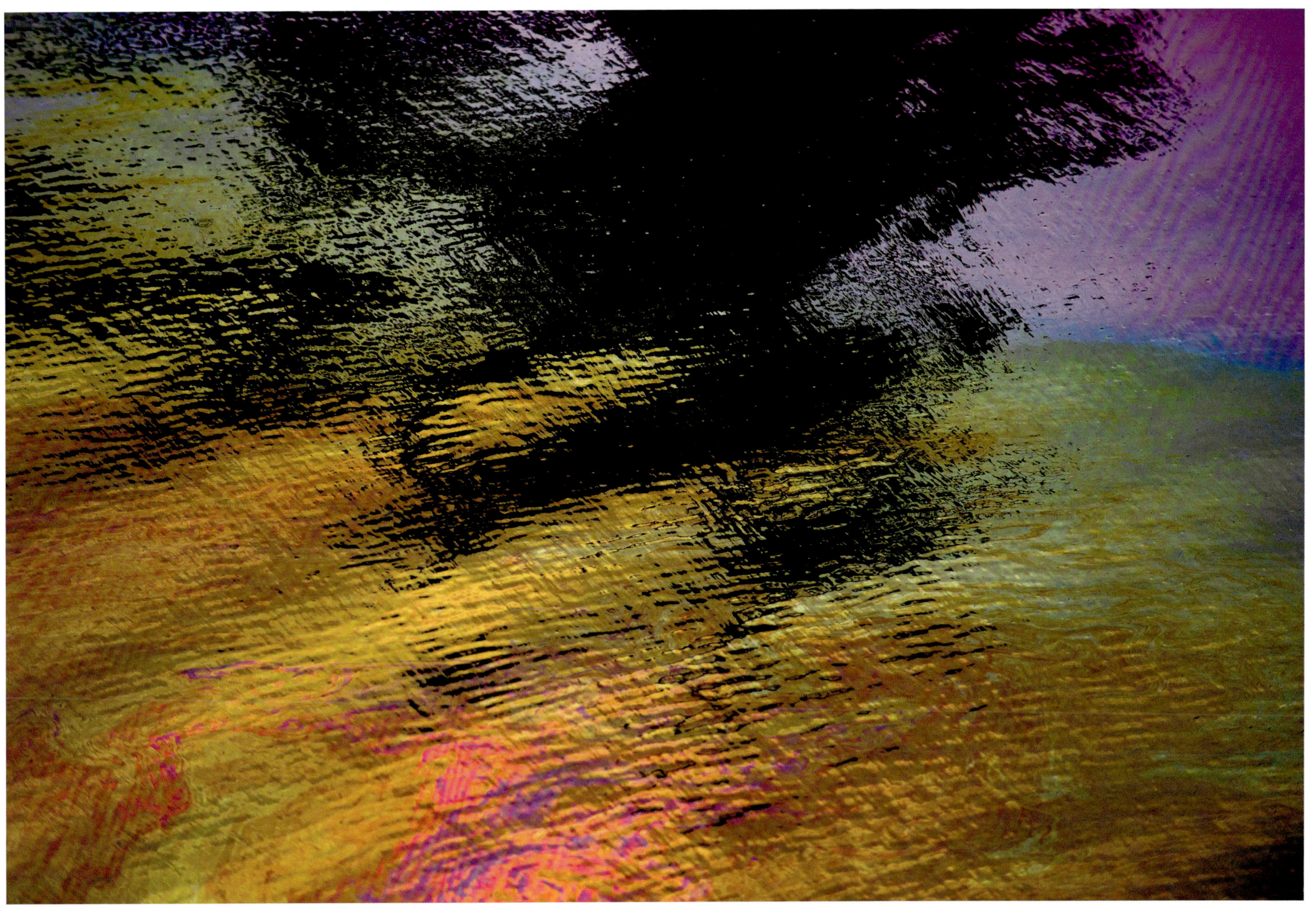

INDEX

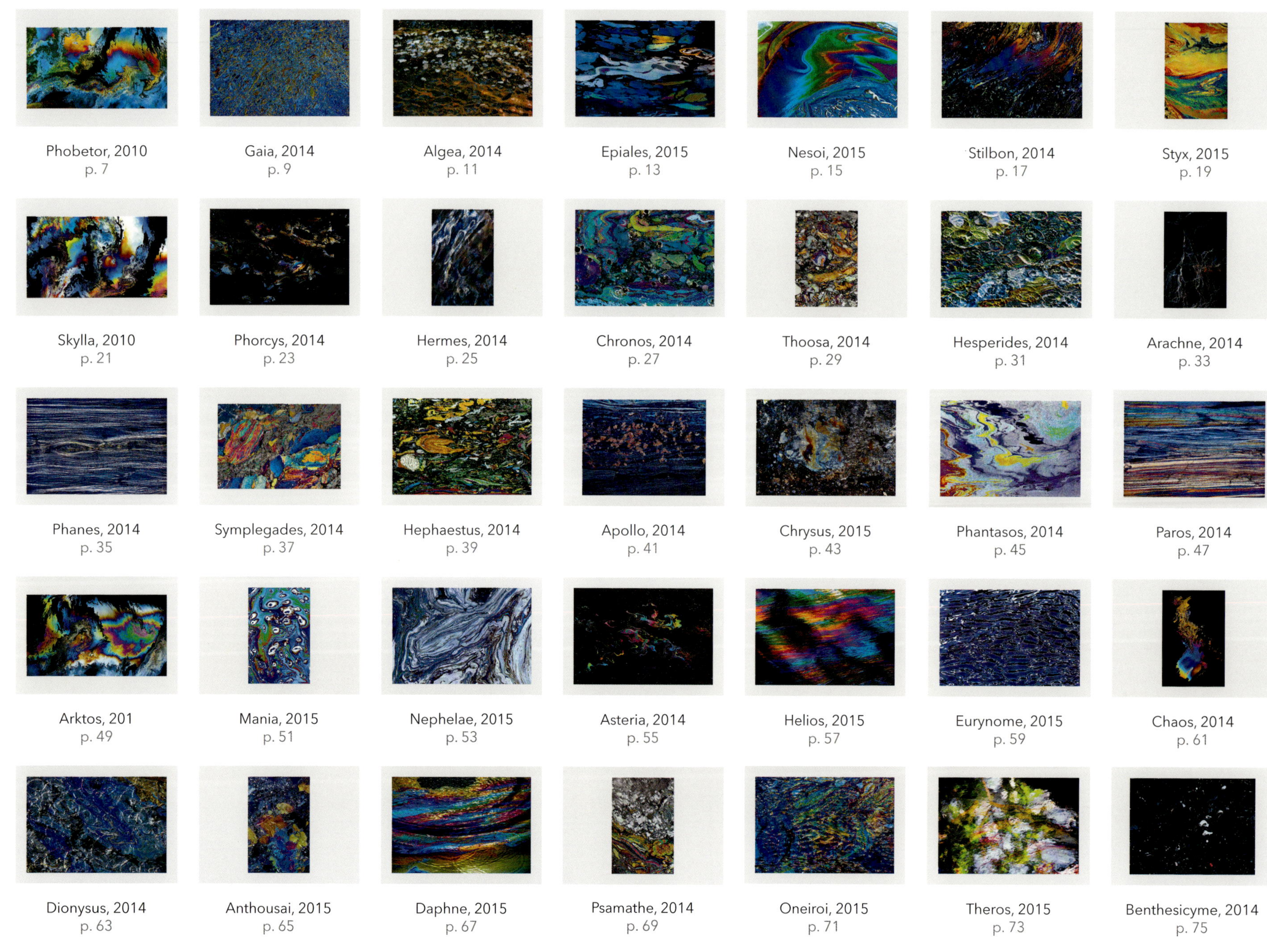

Phobetor, 2010 p. 7	Gaia, 2014 p. 9	Algea, 2014 p. 11	Epiales, 2015 p. 13	Nesoi, 2015 p. 15	Stilbon, 2014 p. 17	Styx, 2015 p. 19
Skylla, 2010 p. 21	Phorcys, 2014 p. 23	Hermes, 2014 p. 25	Chronos, 2014 p. 27	Thoosa, 2014 p. 29	Hesperides, 2014 p. 31	Arachne, 2014 p. 33
Phanes, 2014 p. 35	Symplegades, 2014 p. 37	Hephaestus, 2014 p. 39	Apollo, 2014 p. 41	Chrysus, 2015 p. 43	Phantasos, 2014 p. 45	Paros, 2014 p. 47
Arktos, 201 p. 49	Mania, 2015 p. 51	Nephelae, 2015 p. 53	Asteria, 2014 p. 55	Helios, 2015 p. 57	Eurynome, 2015 p. 59	Chaos, 2014 p. 61
Dionysus, 2014 p. 63	Anthousai, 2015 p. 65	Daphne, 2015 p. 67	Psamathe, 2014 p. 69	Oneiroi, 2015 p. 71	Theros, 2015 p. 73	Benthesicyme, 2014 p. 75

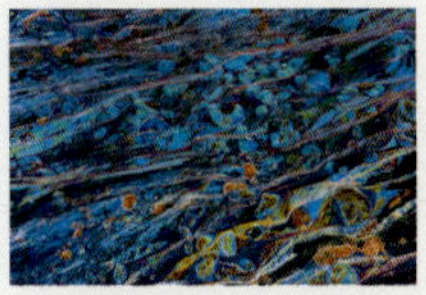

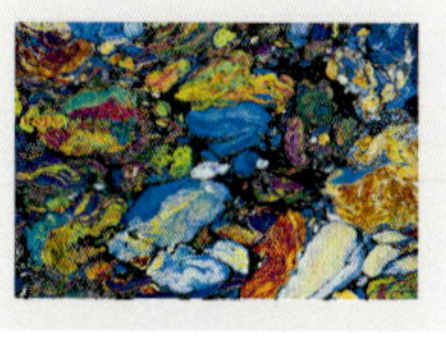

Nereus, 2014
p. 77

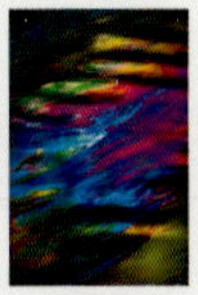

Hypnos, 2015
p. 79

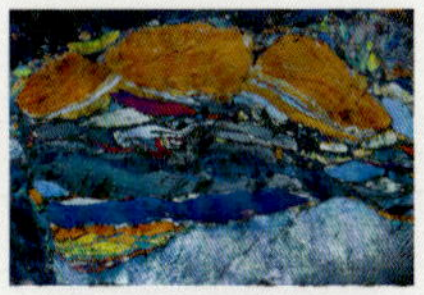

Doris, 2014
p. 81

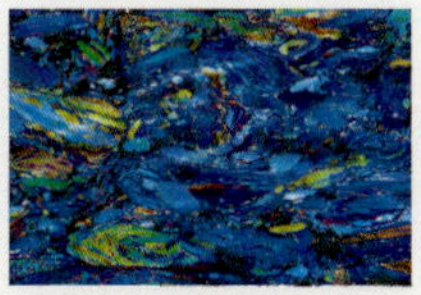

Himeros, 2014
p. 83

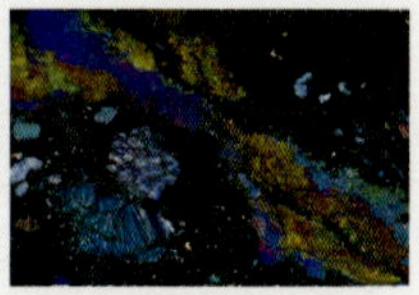

Hecate, 2015
p. 85

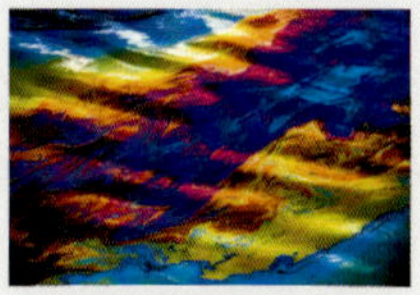

Phlegethon, 2015
p. 87

Nike, 2014
p. 89

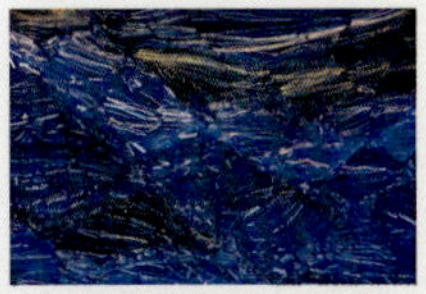

Oceanides, 2014
p. 91

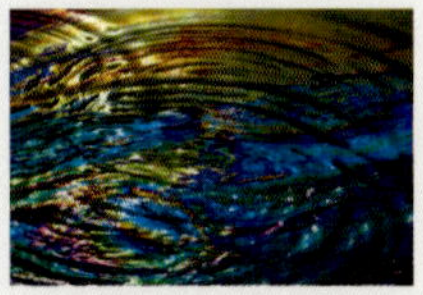

Anatole, 2015
p. 93

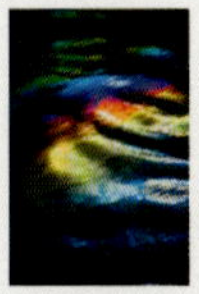

Aura, 2015
p. 95

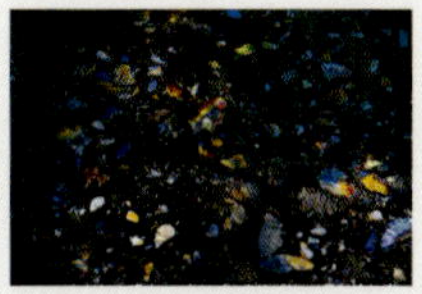

Perses, 2014
p. 97

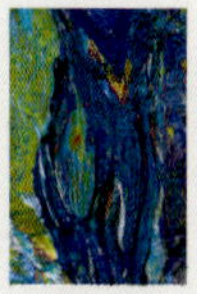

Antheia, 2015
p. 99

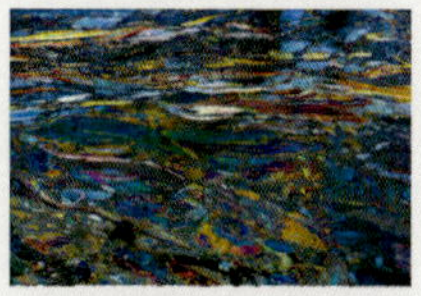

Rhode, 2014
p. 101

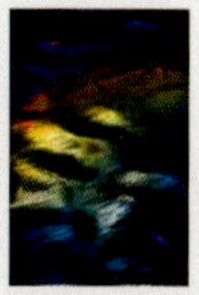

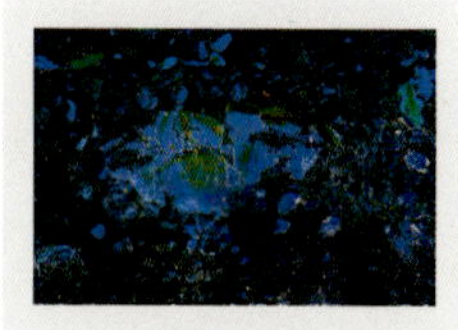

Auge, 2015
p. 103

Erebos, 2015
p. 105

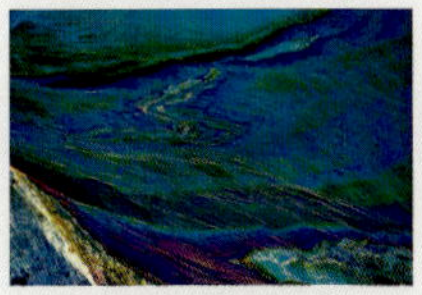

Elar, 2014
p. 107

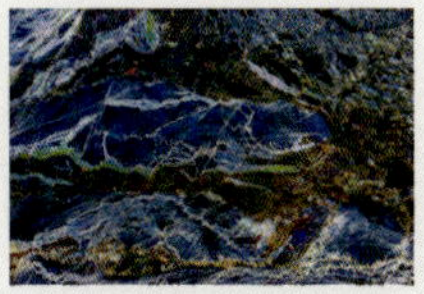

Aphros, 2014
p. 109

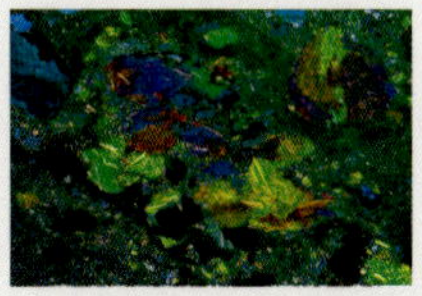

Attis, 2015
p. 111

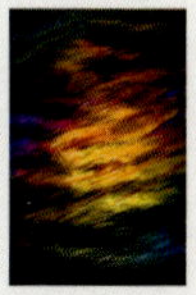

Hyperion, 2015
p. 113

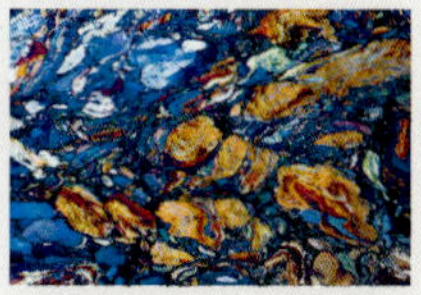

Amphitrite, 2014
p. 115

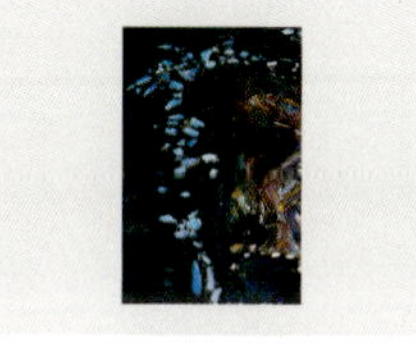

Artemis, 2014
p. 117

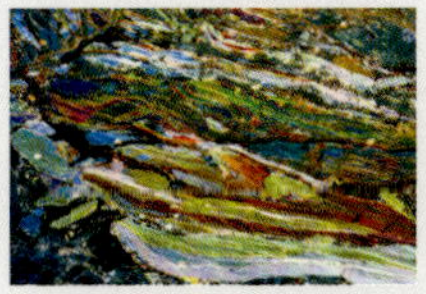

Tartarus, 2014
p. 119

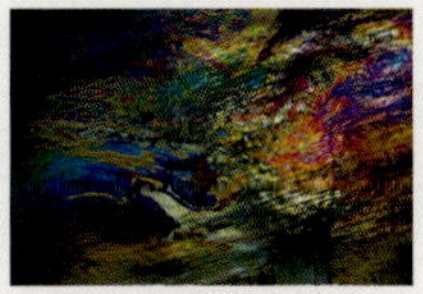

Thassos, 2014
p. 121

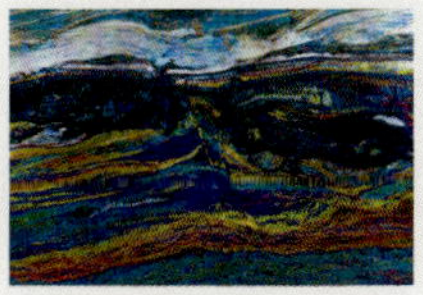

Nemesis, 2015
p. 123

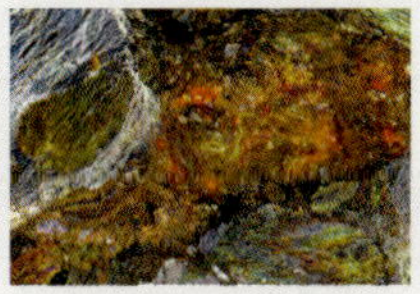

Aether, 2014
p. 125

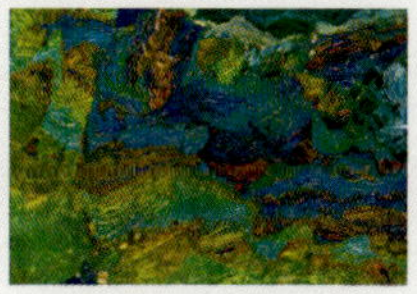

Pistis, 2015
p. 127

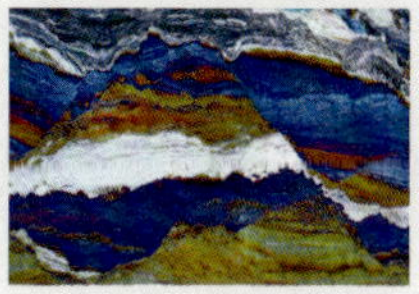

Aetna, 2015
p. 129

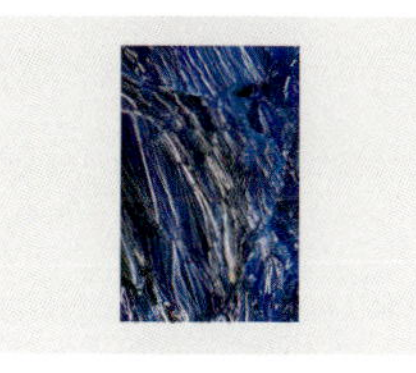

Thetis, 2014
p. 131

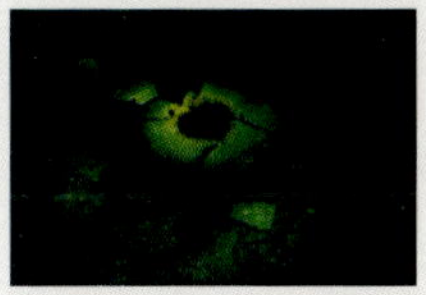

Astraios, 2014
p. 133

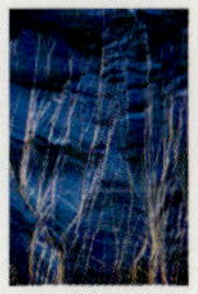

Demeter, 2014
p. 135

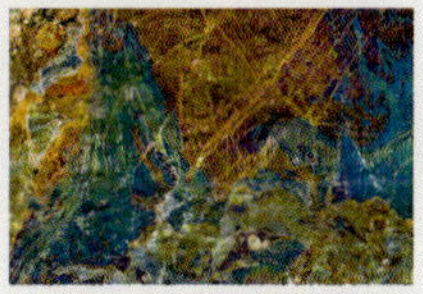

Poseidon, 2014
p. 137

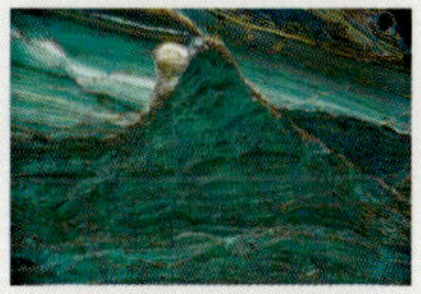

Ceto, 2014
p. 139

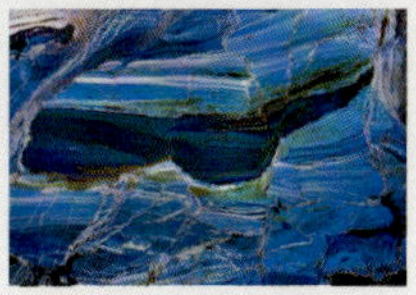

Theia, 2014
p. 141

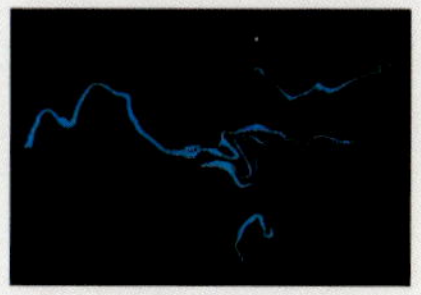

Nyx, 2014
p. 143

Tethys, 2014
p. 145

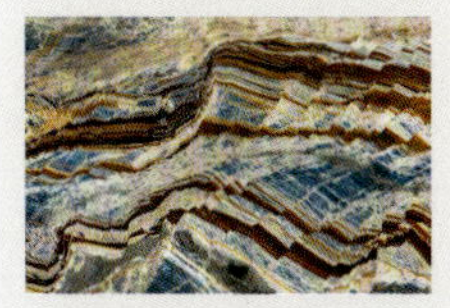

Ourea, 2014
p. 147

Dryades, 2015
p. 149

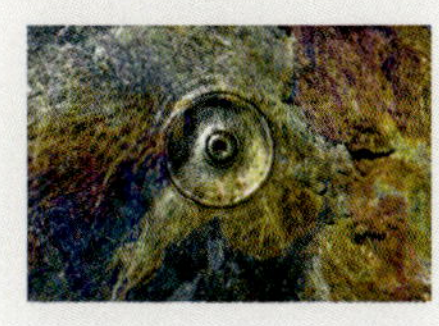

Aphrodite, 2014
p. 151

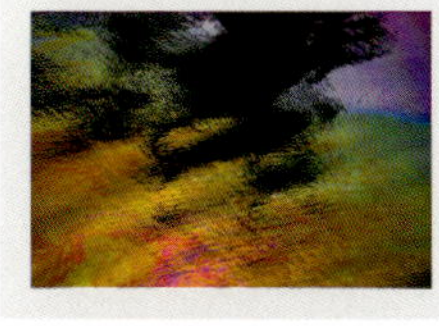

Uranus, 2015
p. 153

GOWANUS WATERS

Photographs © 2016 Steven Hirsch
Introduction © 2016 Jordan G. Teicher

Published in the United States by powerHouse Books,
a division of powerHouse Cultural Entertainment, Inc.
37 Main Street, Brooklyn, NY 11201-1021
telephone 212.604.9074
e-mail: info@powerHouseBooks.com
website: www.powerHouseBooks.com

First edition, 2016

Library of Congress Control Number: 2015955316

Hardcover ISBN 978-1-57687-792-0

Printed by Asia Pacific Offset

Book design by Krzysztof Poluchowicz with Jia Cheng Wu

10 9 8 7 6 5 4 3 2 1

Printed and bound in China